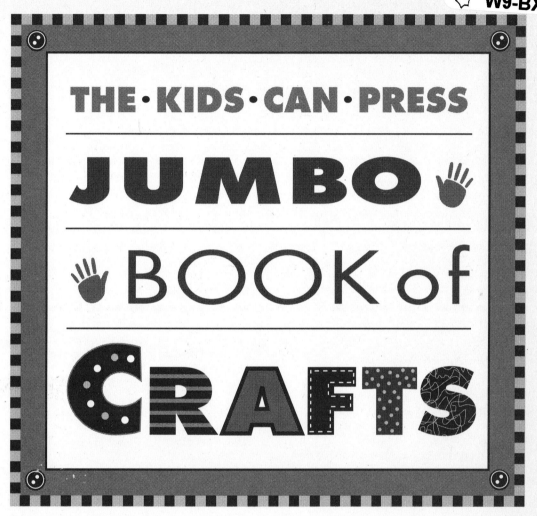

THE · KIDS · CAN · PRESS

JUMBO

BOOK of

CRAFTS

Written by Judy Ann Sadler

Illustrated by Caroline Price

Kids Can Press

A fun-packed, jumbo-sized book
for my fun-packed, jumbo-sized family!

My heartfelt thanks to the following people: Laurie Wark for her ongoing enthusiastic support, encouragement, cheerfulness and top-notch editing skills; Trudee Romanek for making the jumbo step of taking over for Laurie with such grace, good humor and superb attention to detail; Caroline Price for beautifully illustrating each project with boldness and clarity; Karen Powers for using her remarkable artistic and design skills to give this book such a great look; Valerie Hussey and Ricky Englander and everyone else at Kids Can Press for their steadfast dedication to excellence.

First U.S. edition 1998

Text copyright © 1997 by Judy Ann Sadler
Illustrations copyright © 1997 by Caroline Price

Published in Canada by:
Kids Can Press Ltd.
29 Birch Avenue
Toronto, ON M4V 1E2

Published in the U.S. by:
Kids Can Press Ltd.
85 River Rock Drive, Suite 202
Buffalo, NY 14207

Edited by Laurie Wark and Trudee Romanek
Designed by Karen Powers
Printed in Canada by Kromar Printing Limited

CM 97 0 9 8 7 6 5 4 3 2

Canadian Cataloguing in Publication Data

Sadler, Judy Ann, 1959–
    The Kids Can Press jumbo book of crafts

ISBN 1-55074-375-9

1. Handicraft — Juvenile literature. I. Price, Caroline.
II. Title.

TT160.S32 1997   j745.5   C97-930589-6

Contents

⊛ Old-time crafts   160

Things for your room

Here are some super ideas for things you can make for your room. You can welcome (or keep away) others by hanging a collage nameplate on your door. Organize your room with magazine holders, bookends and a decorated bulletin board. Surround yourself with photographs of family and friends in handmade frames. Make your room cozy by stitching up bandanna neck rolls or cushions and T-shirt pillows. Make it restful too by hanging up a traditional dream catcher or a sun-splasher mobile.

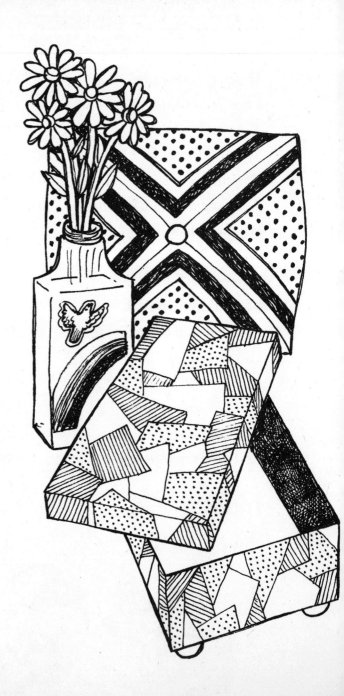

Crafty collage nameplate

If you don't want to put a nail in your door to hang this nameplate on, push a thumbtack into the top ledge of the door. Hang the nameplate from the thumbtack using strong thread or fishing line.

Things you need

- assorted craft supplies (see step 1)
- cardboard
- scissors
- white craft glue
- fabric or felt

- 2 paper clips
- strong tape
- heavy paper
- colored pencils or markers
- strong thread, yarn or fishing line

1 Gather craft supplies such as buttons, beads, pipe cleaners, plastic lacing, yarn, wire, sequins, colored glue, leather cord, ribbon, pencil stubs, nails, screws, nuts and bolts or whatever else you can find. Use these supplies to set out the letters for your nameplate.

2 Cut out a piece of cardboard the right size to hold the letters. If your cardboard is flimsy, cut another piece the same size and glue them together.

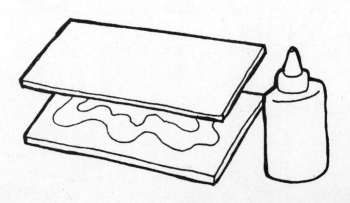

3 Cover the cardboard by gluing on fabric or felt.

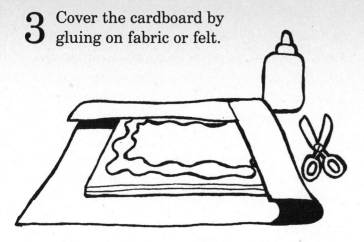

4 Straighten the small inner loop of each paper clip to create a long, thin S shape. Twist these loops sideways and tape them to the bottom of the cardboard so the hooks face forward.

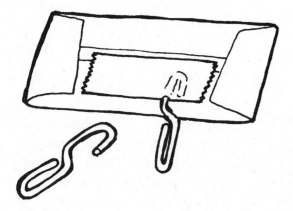

5 Glue the letters onto the cardboard.

6 Cut out pieces of heavy paper for messages. Poke holes in these message boards so they can hang from your nameplate. Make many so you can change them often. Some messages you may want to write are:
Beat it!
Don't even think of coming in
Knock before entering
Quiet: Artist at work
Beware of killer hamster
No adults allowed
Welcome

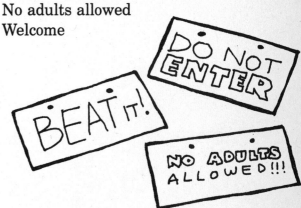

7 Tape yarn, thread or fishing line on your nameplate to hang it on your door.

Découpage magazine and book holder

Make more of these handy holders in different sizes as your magazine and book collection grows.

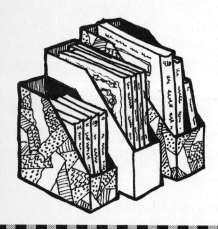

Things you need

- cereal or cracker boxes
- a pencil and a ruler
- scissors
- a foil pie plate or other shallow container
- white craft glue
- a Popsicle stick
- colored comics or other decorative paper
- a plastic bag
- acrylic varnish or a sealer product such as Podgy or Mod Podge and a paintbrush (optional)

1 Cut off the top flaps of the box. (Large cereal boxes will hold magazines and smaller boxes will hold paperback books.)

2 Make a mark 5 cm (2 in.) from the top left corner of the box.

3 Make a mark halfway up the side from the bottom right corner of the box. Draw a straight line to join the two marks.

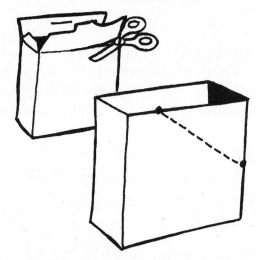

4 Turn the box around and make a mark 5 cm (2 in.) from the top right corner. Make a mark halfway up the box from the bottom left corner. Draw a straight line to join the two marks.

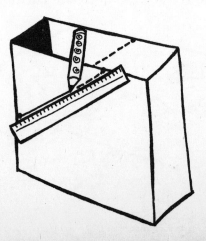

5 Cut along both lines and across the side panel so that your cereal box is now open.

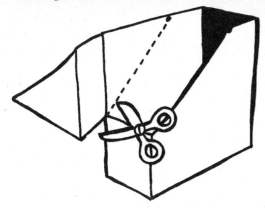

6 With the Popsicle stick, mix 25 mL (2 tbsp.) each of white glue and water in the shallow container.

7 Tear the colored comics or other paper into different-sized strips.

8 Spread a plastic bag on your work surface and place the box on it.

9 Dip a paper strip into the glue mixture. Coat both sides and pull it through your fingers to get rid of any extra glue.

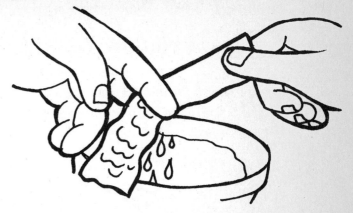

10 Place the strip on the cereal box. Smooth it gently. Continue to dip strips and smooth them onto the box until it is completely covered. You can overlap some of the strips and place them on the box in different directions.

11 Allow the box to dry for a few hours or overnight.

12 If you like, you can paint on a coat of acrylic varnish or sealer to give your magazine holder a shine.

Boxy bookends

These adjustable bookends are perfect for standing books on your desk or bedside table. Decorate them with leftover wallpaper, fabric or paint to match your room.

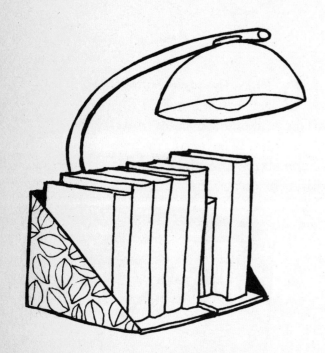

Things you need

- a shoebox
- scissors
- a pencil and a ruler
- tape or white craft glue
- decorative paper, leftover wallpaper, fabric or paint

1 Remove the lid and cut away one long side of your box.

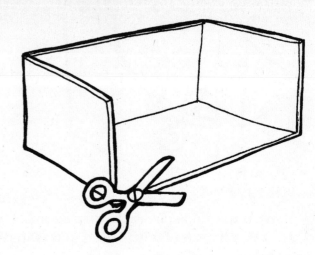

2 Place the box so the cut-away side is facing you. Mark the center of the opposite long side along its bottom edge.

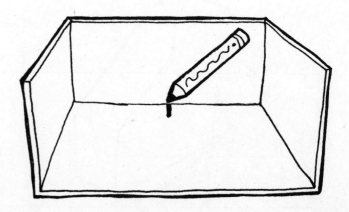

3 Draw a line from the center mark straight towards you. Draw another line from the top left back corner to the center mark, and a third line from the top right back corner to the center mark.

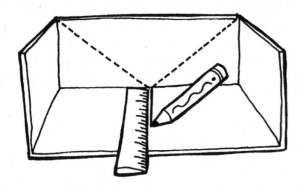

4 Cut along each of these lines and remove the triangle of cardboard. If your bookends look too deep, trim some cardboard along the front and side edges.

5 Glue or tape down any loose edges. Decorate the two sides of your bookends with colorful paper, fabric or paint. Or follow the instructions on page 10 for how to decorate with découpage.

6 When your bookends are finished, tuck one inside the other so that the cut edge of one bookend is pushed against the inside edge of the other bookend. This is the shortest position for your adjustable bookends. As you add more books, simply pull the bookends farther apart.

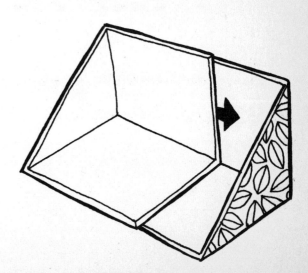

Decorated bulletin board

Make this board any shape you like. If you don't have much wall space, make a small one — it'll still hold lots of notes.

Things you need

- corrugated cardboard
- a pencil
- scissors
- white craft glue
- real felt (not acrylic) or fabric such as denim
- supplies for decorating (see step 6)
- a hammer
- 2 or 3 nails

1 Draw a shape for your bulletin board on the cardboard. Geometric shapes work well, but you could also try a football, dog or race car.

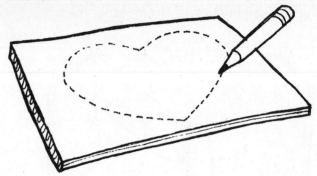

2 Cut out the shape, trace it on more cardboard and cut out the second one.

3 Glue the two cutouts together. Smooth them all over with your hands.

4 Use a pencil to trace the shape onto a piece of felt or fabric. If your felt or fabric is dark, use a piece of chalk or a dry sliver of soap to trace it. Cut it out.

5 Spread a thin layer of glue all over the cardboard and smooth the felt over it.

6 Decorate around the edges of your bulletin board. Glue on shells, buttons, beads, braided yarn, ribbon, silk flowers, photographs, magazine pictures or whatever else you can find.

7 Ask an adult to help you nail it to the wall. Use straight pins, push pins or thumbtacks to fasten on your notes.

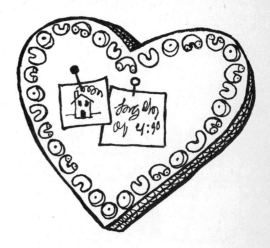

More ideas

If you already have a bulletin board, jazz up the frame with paint or any of the other decorating ideas in step 6.

Uncanny desk organizer

Use tall cans for rulers, pens and pencils, a small can for markers and glue sticks, and a short can for erasers and paper clips.

Things you need

- an assortment of clean, label-free cans
- cloth tape or masking tape
- scissors
- white craft glue
- supplies for decorating (see step 2)
- waxed paper

1 Tape over the tops of the cans so there are no sharp edges.

2 Decorate the cans using one or more of the following ideas. The cans don't all need to be decorated in the same style.

- Wrap and glue yarn, ribbon or fabric around a can.

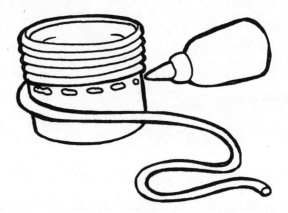

- Cut a piece of self-adhesive vinyl, leftover wallpaper or shelf paper a little longer than the height of the can. Wrap it around the can so it extends above the top. Cut slits in the vinyl and smooth it to the inside.

• Glue plain paper onto a can and decorate it with drawings, paint or stenciling (see page 182). Seal it with a coat of Mod Podge, acrylic varnish or watered-down glue.

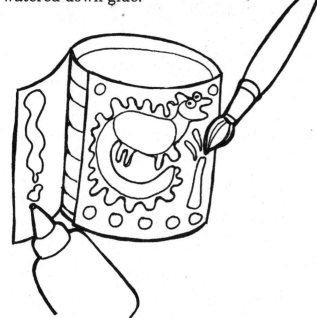

• Cover a can with a collage of magazine pictures of your favorite sports players, singers or actors, or any other magazine pictures you find interesting.

3 Place the decorated cans on a sheet of waxed paper. Arrange them so the tall ones are in the back and the short ones are in the front.

4 Glue the cans together along the sides. Allow them to dry on the waxed paper. If you can't glue them together because the sides don't touch, glue them onto a cardboard base which you can trim after the glue is dry. Or, tie them together with ribbon, twine or a strip of fabric.

More ideas

⊙ Make a desk organizer out of decorated cardboard tubes instead of cans. Glue them onto a cardboard base, which you can trim after the glue is dry.

⊙ Make an organizer with cans or tubes all the same height. Position it on its side on your desk.

Bandanna cushion

Here's a simple way to make a terrific pillow out of a bandanna. Use it on your bed or as a chair pad.

Things you need

- a square bandanna
- pins
- a needle and thread to match the bandanna
- scissors
- a pencil
- polyester fiber stuffing
- 2 buttons
- a dollmaker's needle (long and strong)

1 Fold the bandanna in half with the good sides together. Pin both short sides.

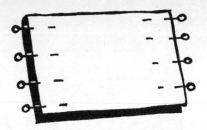

2 Thread your needle with about two arm lengths of thread. Double the thread and knot it. Backstitch (see page 202) each short side closed. Remove the pins as you sew. As you finish each side, make a couple of small stitches on the same spot and cut, knot and trim the threads.

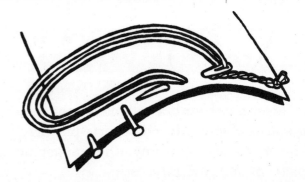

3 Use your pencil to mark the center of the long edge. (You can fold it in half to find the center point.) Turn the folded bandanna over and mark the center of the other long edge.

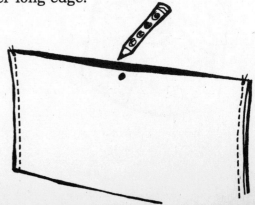

4 Open the bandanna by holding one marked edge in each hand and pulling gently in opposite directions. This should make the bandanna into a diamond shape.

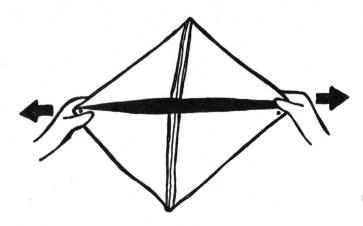

5 Start pinning this long seam together. As you reach the center, try to match the seams you have already sewn. Pin until you are about three-quarters of the way to the other end.

6 Backstitch the seam until you reach the end of the pins. Remove all the pins.

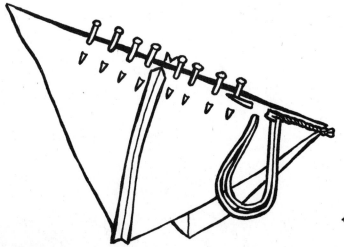

7 Turn the bandanna right side out and stuff it. Be sure to get stuffing in each corner, too.

8 Stitch the seam closed. At the end of the seam, make a couple of small stitches on the same spot, poke the needle through the cushion to the other side and trim the threads.

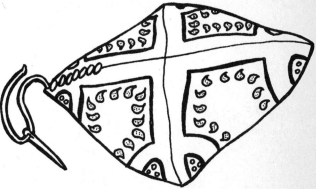

9 To sew on the buttons, use a piece of doubled thread in a dollmaker's needle, knotted at the end. Poke the needle up through the center of the cushion, through a button hole, down through the other hole and through the pillow again. Bring the needle through the other button, up through the second hole, back through the pillow and through the first button. Keep sewing until both buttons are on tightly. Make a couple of small stitches under one of the buttons and cut, knot and trim the threads.

Stuffed T-shirt pillow

Have you ever had a special T-shirt that you wished you hadn't outgrown? Here's a way to recycle that shirt into a pillow so you can keep enjoying it.

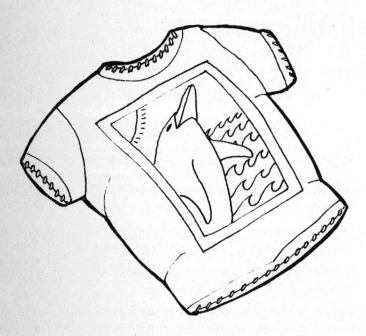

Things you need

- an old T-shirt
- thread or embroidery floss
- scissors
- a needle
- polyester fiber stuffing

1 Use an overcast stitch as shown to close the neck, sleeves and half the bottom of your T-shirt.

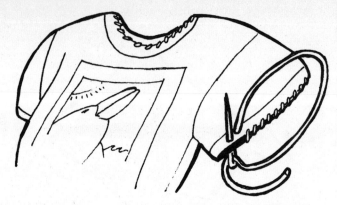

2 Put stuffing in the sleeves, around the neck and in the rest of the T-shirt so it is plump.

3 Use the overcast stitch to close the rest of the bottom of the T-shirt.

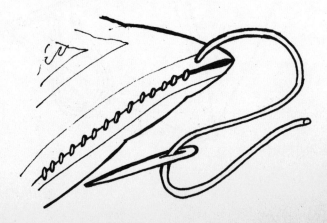

Bandanna neck roll

Bandannas come in many colors and sizes. Choose one that will look nice on your bed.

Things you need

- a bandanna
- pins
- scissors
- a needle and thread
- ribbon
- clean, old towels and rags or polyester fiber stuffing

1 Fold the bandanna in half, with the good sides together, and pin it. Don't worry if the edges do not match.

2 Backstitch (see page 202) the long edge. Remove the pins. Turn the bandanna right side out.

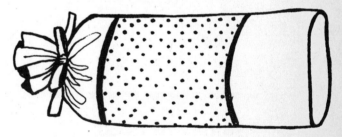

3 Tie ribbon into a double-knot bow to close one end of the pillow.

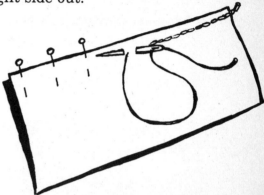

4 Roll up the rags as smoothly as you can and slide them into the bandanna pillowcase, or use the polyester fiber stuffing. Tie the other end closed with ribbon.

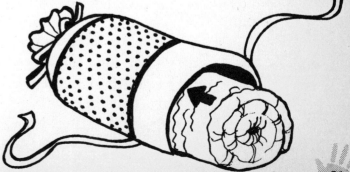

Treasure box

This treasure box can be used for everything from CDs and cassettes to jewelry and vacation souvenirs. A small box from a child's pair of shoes is a good one to use.

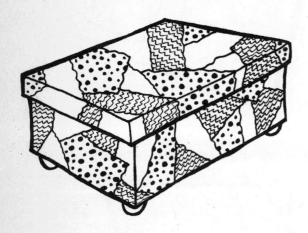

1 Cut or tear the wrapping paper in various sizes and shapes.

2 Mix together equal amounts of glue and water in the plastic tub. Start with 15 mL (1 tbsp.) of each and mix up more if you need it. Stir it thoroughly with the Popsicle stick.

3 Spread waxed paper on your work surface. Brush an area of the shoebox with the glue mixture. Smooth on a piece of wrapping paper. Make sure the paper is completely glued down.

Things you need

- scraps of wrapping paper or magazine and catalog pictures
- scissors
- a yogurt or margarine tub
- white craft glue
- a Popsicle stick
- waxed paper

- a shoebox with a lid (If you don't have one, ask at a shoe store.)
- a craft paintbrush
- glitter, beads, sequins, ribbon or lace for decorating
- 4 wooden beads
- water-based varnish (optional)

4 Keep brushing on glue and smoothing on paper until the box is covered. Cover the lid, too.

5 If you'd like to decorate your box with sequins, beads or ribbon, brush on more glue and add them.

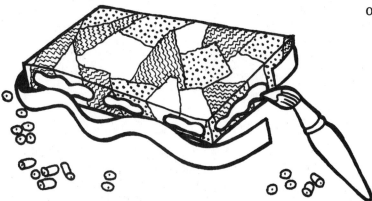

6 Glue a wooden bead on each of the four bottom corners to make feet. Allow the box to dry overnight.

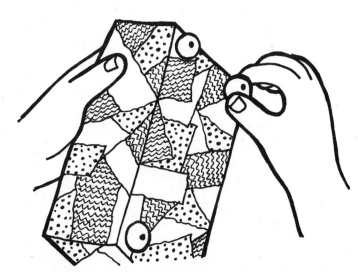

7 When the box is dry, you can brush on a coat of water-based varnish for a little extra shine and protection.

More ideas

● For a jewelry box, line the inside of the box with fabric or felt. Cut cardboard strips to fit across the box to make dividers and cover them with fabric or felt, too.

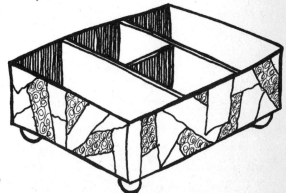

● Personalize the treasure box to give as a gift. For a sports fan, cover it with pictures from sports magazines. Or use pictures from nature or fashion magazines. You could even glue a special photograph onto the lid.

Découpage vase

Try many shapes and sizes of bottles for this vase. Instead of doing one cutout on the bottle, you could also try covering it completely with cut or torn pictures.

1 Remove the labels from the bottle and make sure the bottle is clean and dry.

2 Cut out a picture from wrapping paper, wallpaper, a magazine, a greeting card or fabric.

3 Glue the cutout onto the bottle. (You may want to thin the glue with a little water and brush it on the cutout.) Make sure every edge is glued down. Press out any air bubbles. Prick any tiny ones with a pin.

Things you need

- a glass or clear plastic bottle, such as a salad-dressing bottle
- paper or fabric for a cutout
- scissors
- white craft glue
- a paintbrush
- acrylic varnish or a sealer product such as Mod Podge

4 Remove any extra glue around the edges with a wet cloth, or scratch it off if it has already dried. Allow the cutout to dry.

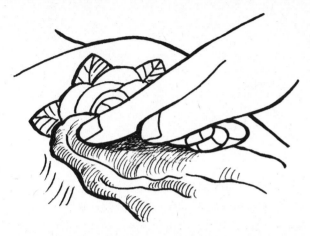

5 Brush over the cutout with sealer, acrylic varnish or watered-down glue. Be careful not to brush too far beyond the edges of the cutout. Keep it tidy. Allow the vase to dry. Apply another sealer coat if you think it needs it.

6 Arrange fresh, silk or dried flowers in the vase. If you ever need to clean it, rinse the inside quickly rather than letting it soak.

More ideas

○ Instead of using a bottle, try decorating an inexpensive plain vase or the base of an old lamp.

○ For something different, dip yarn or thin jute into a mixture of white glue and water. Start at the top and wind the yarn around the bottle until it is completely covered.

Dream catcher

Native legends tell us that the web in a dream catcher holds good dreams while allowing the bad ones to disappear through the center hole. Hang yours near your bed for sweet dreams.

1 Triple knot the end of your waxed thread onto the brass ring, leaving a short tail.

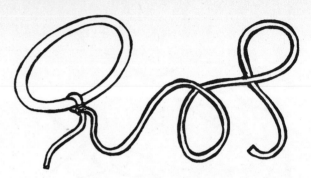

2 Pull the thread taut across the ring about 3 cm (1 ¼ in.) from the knot. Bring the thread behind the ring and pull it through the space between the taut thread and the ring.

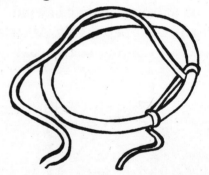

3 Continue around the ring until you have nine points. Adjust them so they are evenly spaced.

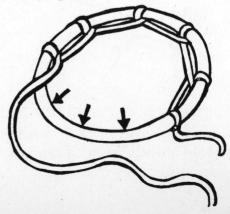

Things you need

- a brass ring 10 cm (4 in.) in diameter
- 2 m (6 ½ ft.) of waxed linen thread or artificial sinew (available at craft supply stores)
- scissors
- E beads
- thick beige or brown yarn or jute
- pony beads
- colorful feathers
- white craft glue

4 When you get back to the starting-point knot, wind the working thread around the knot a couple of times.

5 From behind, bring the working thread through the first loop on the ring. Continue around the circle, keeping the thread tight.

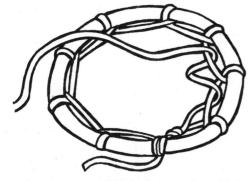

6 As you go, thread on a few E beads. Use beads to match your room or perhaps use red, yellow, black and white to symbolize all the nations of the world.

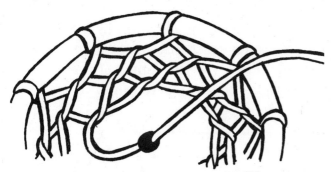

7 When your central circle is small, securely knot your thread and weave it around a few threads. Trim it.

8 Tie the yarn or jute onto the brass ring. Wind the yarn around the ring, covering the yarn end and the waxed thread tail. Tie off the yarn and dab a little glue on it to keep it in place.

9 Cut three pieces of yarn, each 40 cm (16 in.) long. Tie one on the bottom of the ring and one on each side. Thread a couple of pony beads on each yarn end. Knot the thread to keep them on. Thread feathers into each set of beads. Add a little glue if the feathers feel loose.

10 Tie a loop to the top of the dream catcher to hang it up. Sweet dreams!

Fabric frame

Make this frame as simple or as fancy as you like. You may find that a colorfully decorated frame looks better with a plain photograph, and a plain frame looks better with a colorful photograph.

Things you need

- corrugated or other sturdy cardboard
- a pencil and a ruler
- newspaper or more cardboard
- an X-acto knife
- fabric or wrapping paper
- white craft glue
- scissors

1 Place the cardboard on newspaper or other cardboard so you don't cut through to the table top. Carefully cut out two rectangles with an X-acto knife. Cut one 15 cm x 20 cm (6 in. x 8 in.), and the other 13 cm x 18 cm (5 in. x 7 in.). These will make a frame for a 10 cm x 15 cm (4 in. x 6 in.) photograph. If you need to, change the measurements to suit your photograph.

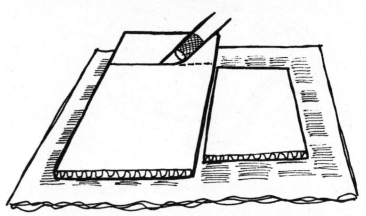

2 Mark lines 3 cm (1¼ in.) in from all four sides on the large rectangle. Carefully cut away the center of the rectangle using the X-acto knife.

3 Cut a piece of fabric or paper 20 cm x 25 cm (8 in. x 10 in.). Place it good side down on the table.

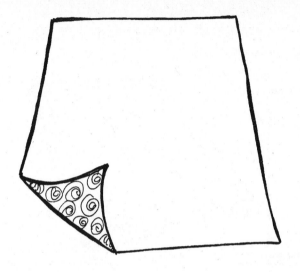

4 Spread a thin layer of glue on one side of the cardboard frame. Center it, glue side down, on the fabric. Gently smooth it with your hands.

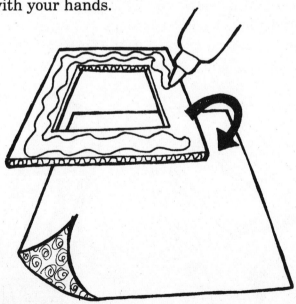

5 Using the point of your scissors or the X-acto knife, poke a hole in the center of the fabric. Cut the fabric from the center hole to each corner to make an X.

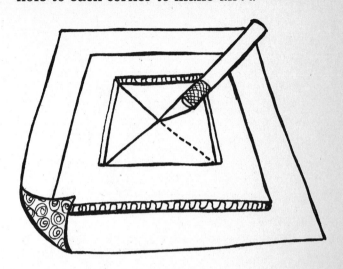

6 Trim the inside fabric to make a small rectangular opening. Also cut away the points of the outside corners of the fabric.

Continued on next page

7 Glue the inside fabric flaps to the back of the frame. Then glue the outside corner areas and finish by gluing the side fabric flaps. Let the frame dry.

9 When the frame is dry, cut a piece of cardboard about 4 cm x 18 cm (1½ in. x 7 in.). Bend the top 4 cm (1½ in.) over. Glue this bent area to the top of the back of the frame so that the end of the stand is even with the end of the frame. Allow it to dry.

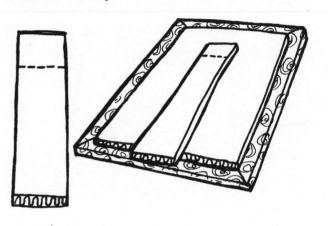

8 Apply glue to the outer edges of the top one-third of the small cardboard rectangle. Center it on the back of the frame. Place a heavy book on the frame and allow it to dry.

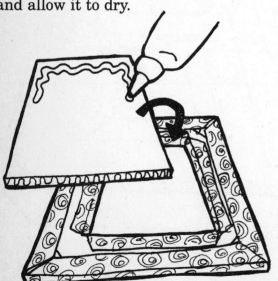

10 When it is dry, gently lift the back of the frame and slide in a photograph. Stand the frame up. If the stand slides backwards, tape or glue a piece of ribbon or yarn from the stand to the back of the frame.

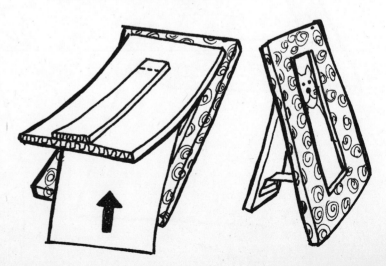

More ideas

● Instead of covering the frame with fabric or paper, try squirting a pattern of glue lines all around the frame. Allow it to dry overnight. Paint over the glue and frame with gold or silver acrylic craft paint.

● Make creative clay shapes (see page 138) such as stars, hearts, sports equipment, animals or other designs to suit the photograph or your room. Decorate them with paint and glue them onto the frame.

● Decorate the frame with seashells, buttons and beads, pressed flowers (see page 86) or découpage (see page 10) with tissue paper, used postage stamps, wrapping paper or magazine cutouts. Glue on dried or silk flowers or ribbon and lace. If you are using the frame for a vacation photograph, cover it with a map of the area where the picture was taken.

● All the above ideas can be used on store-bought ready-to-decorate frames, too.

Picture cube

Photographs, artwork or magazine pictures all look terrific displayed on a picture cube. Create many cubes in different sizes so you can make a mobile or stack them on a table.

Things you need

- blank index cards or other heavy paper or thin cardboard
- a pencil and a ruler
- scissors
- white craft glue
- a hole punch
- yarn

1 Measure and cut out a square on an index card. Make it 5 cm (2 in.) square for a small cube, 6 cm (2 1/4 in.) for a medium cube or 10 cm (4 in.) for a large cube.

2 Use your square as a pattern to cut out six squares. Save your pattern in case you want to make more cubes.

3 Decorate the squares with drawings or messages, or glue on magazine pictures or photographs.

4 Use your hole punch to make a hole in the four corners of each square.

5 Tie two of the squares together, top and bottom, with yarn. Knot the yarn and trim off the ends. Add two more squares so you have four in a row. Tie the first and the fourth together to form a large, open square.

7 Repeat for the other end to close the cube. Tuck all the knots inside the cube so they don't show. Sit the cube on a shelf or tie on a piece of yarn so you can hang up your cube.

6 Place another square on top and tie it at each corner with yarn threaded through a top corner hole and each of the two side holes.

■■■■■■■■■■■■■■■■■■■■■■■■■■■

More ideas

⊗ Cut up used greeting cards to make small festive cubes that can be hung on a tree or in a doorway.

⊗ Cover the sides of the cube with self-adhesive plastic to protect the pictures.

Sun-splasher mobile

Hang this mobile where it can reflect sunshine and it will splash color around your room.

1 If you are using plastic other than a bottle, go to step 3. Otherwise, poke into the top of the bottle with the end of your scissors or an X-acto knife.

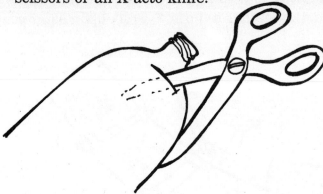

2 Ask an adult to help you cut the top and bottom off the bottle and cut it up the center. Handle the plastic carefully in case there are any jagged edges. The plastic may curl up, so hold it down or cut it into pieces before you begin to draw.

Things you need

- a clear plastic bottle or other clear, thin plastic
- scissors
- permanent markers
- a large safety pin
- an eraser
- fishing line or fine thread
- clear nail polish
- skewers, fine dowel or other sticks

3 Plan what you'd like your mobile to look like. Draw shapes on the plastic, color them with permanent markers and cut them out. You should have at least five shapes and they can be different sizes.

4 Make a small hole in each cutout shape by placing it on the eraser and poking through it with the safety pin.

5 Tie a different length of fishing line onto each shape. Dab each knot with nail polish to secure it.

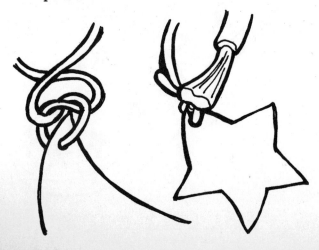

6 Ask someone to hold your two sticks in an X shape. Tie them together with line or thread. Add a loop for hanging up your mobile.

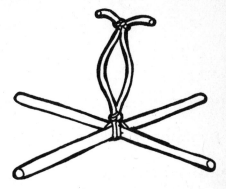

7 Tie the shapes onto the sticks. Try to balance the mobile by adjusting the position of the shapes as well as sliding the sticks a little.

8 When you are pleased with how your mobile looks, trim the threads and dab nail polish on the knots. Hang up your mobile in a sunny spot.

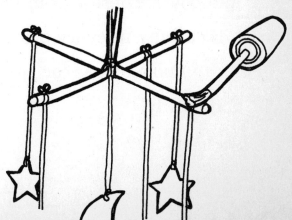

Things to wear

This section is packed full of ideas for decorating *yourself!* Whether it's a wildly printed T-shirt or a finely beaded bracelet, you'll have a one-of-a-kind wearable piece of art. Roll colorful paper beads and turn them into unique earrings. Cover a hair band with your favorite fabric. Tie-dye a T-shirt, socks or underwear. Make bracelets out of embroidery floss, beads or buttons. Decorate a hat or barrette with homemade flowers and bows. There's room for your own creativity in every project. Remember to make extras for your friends and family!

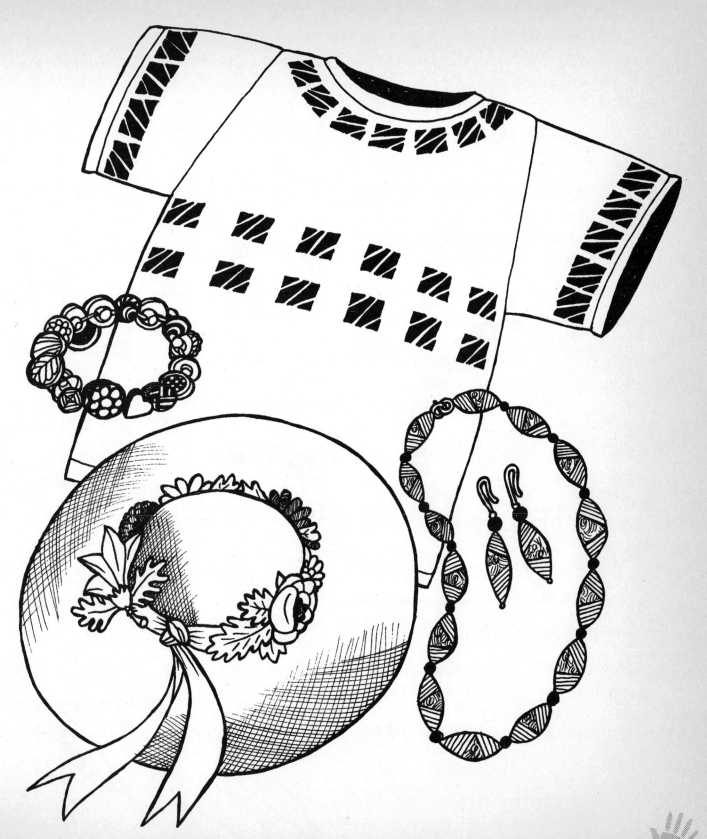

Beaded jewelry

Make a simple bracelet, necklace, choker or anklet using seed beads, or experiment by combining different types of beads in many sizes and colors.

Things you need

- beading thread or fishing line
- scissors
- a clasp (optional)

- seed beads, E beads or larger beads
- a beading needle (optional)
- clear nail polish

1 Cut a piece of thread the length you want your finished piece of jewelry to be plus 25 cm (10 in.).

2 Use a triple knot to tie on a clasp about 10 cm (4 in.) from the end of the thread. Do not trim the thread. Anchor a bead onto the end if you are not using a clasp.

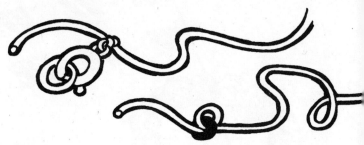

3 Decide on a pattern and start threading on beads, with or without a needle.

4 Measure the bracelet or necklace around your wrist or neck and continue the pattern until it fits. Try to end the pattern so it matches the beginning.

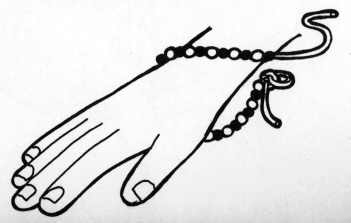

5 If you are using a clasp, tie a ring or tag onto the other end, making the knot as close to the ring as you can. If you're not using a clasp, knot the ends together.

6 Draw the thread end back through the last several beads on the bracelet. Trim the thread. Do the same for the other end.

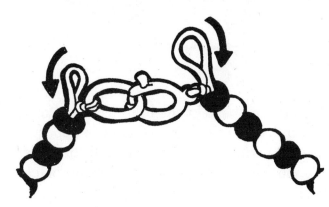

7 Secure the knots by dabbing them with nail polish.

More ideas

🔘 Thread beads larger than seed beads onto elastic cord for a bracelet that slips easily over your hand and fits snugly on your wrist.

🔘 Use waxed linen (or some other type of thick cord or yarn) with beads larger than seed beads. Tie knots between the beads for an interesting necklace or bracelet variation.

Beaded circle bracelet

Fishing line without a needle works well for this bracelet. If you don't have any, use beading thread with a needle on each end.

Things you need

- 1 m (3 ft.) of fishing line
- a clasp (optional)
- seed beads in 2 colors
- scissors
- clear nail polish

1 If you are using a clasp, thread and knot it onto the center of your fishing line.

2 Thread three beads of the same color onto each end of the line. Thread one more bead of the same color onto one of the ends. Poke through it from the opposite direction with the other end. Pull the ends in opposite directions so that the seven beads form a circle. Center the circle on your line.

3 Put one bead of the other color onto one end. Poke through it from the opposite direction with the other end. Pull the ends in opposite directions until this bead meets the first ones.

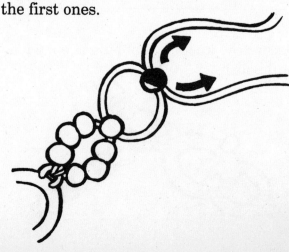

4 Thread three same-colored beads onto each end. Thread one more on one end and poke through it from the opposite direction with the other end. Pull the ends in opposite directions to form a circle made of eight beads.

6 Fasten on the ring end of the clasp. If you are not using a clasp, simply tie the end into the first circle. Poke the ends back through the closest beads and trim them. Secure the knots with nail polish.

5 Change colors and continue making eight-bead circles until your bracelet fits.

More ideas

- Make this bracelet in one color or in more than two colors.

- Make bracelets out of circles made from four or six beads, or try circles larger than eight beads.

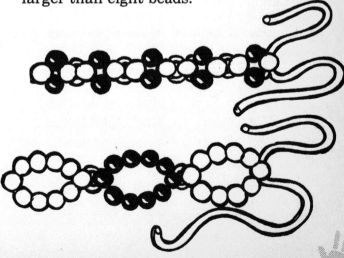

Daisy-chain bracelet

These instructions use green, yellow and black seed beads. You can use any three colors; just change the colors named in the instructions to suit you. Use at least double the amount of fishing line to make a necklace.

Things you need

- 1 m (3 ft.) of beading thread or fishing line
- a clasp and ring (optional)
- green, yellow and black seed beads
- a beading needle
- scissors
- clear nail polish

1 If you are using a clasp, tie it 10 cm (4 in.) from the end of the thread. If you are not using a clasp, anchor a green bead 10 cm (4 in.) from the end.

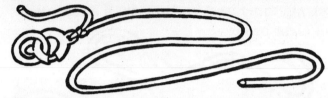

2 Thread on three green beads (two if you're not using a clasp) and eight yellow ones.

3 Bring the thread through the first yellow bead you put on. Go through it in the same direction, from the side closest to the green beads. Pull the thread all the way through to make a circle and gently slide the circle as close to the green beads as possible.

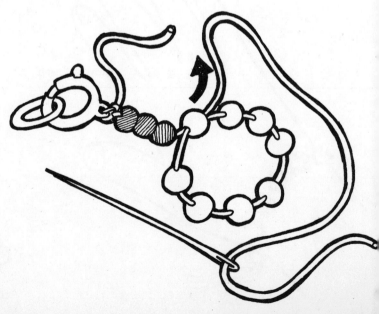

4 Thread on one black bead. Bring the thread through the yellow bead directly across from the first yellow one you threaded on, again from the same direction.

7 Tie the ends together or tie on the ring end of the clasp. Draw the ends through the last several beads, trim them and secure the knots with nail polish.

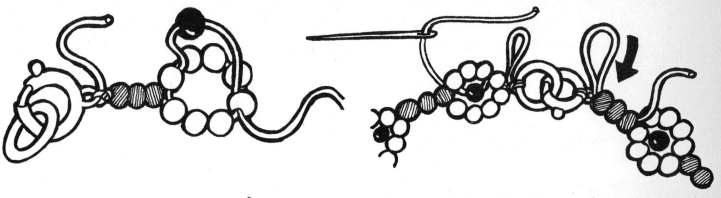

5 Pull on the thread and adjust the daisy so that the black bead is in the center.

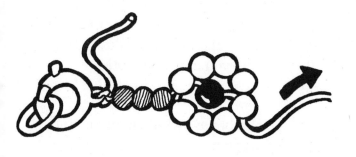

6 Thread on three more green beads and eight more yellow beads. Repeat from step 3 until the bracelet fits.

More ideas

⊙ Instead of putting three green beads between each daisy, put four or more. Or leave them out altogether for non-stop daisies.

⊙ Use an E bead instead of a seed bead for the center of the daisy. Or make the bracelet completely with E beads. Use six beads instead of eight to form each flower.

Rolled beads

Rolled beads are easy to make, very inexpensive and they can be as fun or fancy as you wish. A clothing catalog is a great place to look for colorful pictures to use for beads.

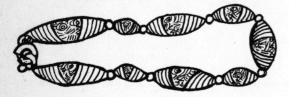

Things you need

- a sheet of paper
- a pencil and a ruler
- scissors
- white craft glue
- round toothpicks
- lightweight cardboard or plastic
- shiny, colorful magazine or catalog pages or covers

1 Fold the sheet of paper in half. Make a dot on the folded edge 15 cm (6 in.) up from the bottom. Make another dot 1.5 cm (5/8 in.) from the fold along the bottom edge. Join these dots with a ruler.

2 Cut along this line. Open the paper and glue it onto a piece of lightweight cardboard or plastic. Cut the shape out. This is your pattern.

3 Use your pattern to trace triangles onto the magazine or catalog pages.

4 Cut out the triangles. You will need about 25 triangles to make a necklace. Cut out extras so you can make other things, too.

5 To make the beads, wind the wide end of the triangle around a toothpick. Guide the paper as you roll so the point of the triangle ends up in the middle of the bead.

6 Spread some glue on the last 3 cm (1 in.) of the triangle and smooth it down flat. Hold it in place for a moment as the glue dries.

7 Carefully take the bead off the toothpick and wind on another one.

More ideas

⚫ Cut longer, wider or narrower triangles and experiment with different shapes, too.

⚫ Make rolled beads out of color comics or used wrapping paper. Finish these beads with acrylic varnish or Mod Podge while they are on the toothpick. Stick them into a potato, sponge or Plasticine to dry.

⚫ Cut a length of ribbon or fabric 8 to 15 cm (3 to 6 in.) long. Spread a thin layer of glue on the wrong side and wind it, right side showing, onto a straw. If it doesn't come off the straw when it is dry, cut off the straw ends and leave the straw inside.

Rolled-bead earrings

Things you need

- 2 head or eye pins
- 2 small beads
- 2 rolled beads
- needlenose pliers
- 2 earring wires

1 Slide a small bead and a rolled bead onto each pin.

2 Use the pliers to bend the top of each pin into a loop.

3 Hang the pins on earring wires. For a variation, try hanging more than one beaded pin on each earring wire.

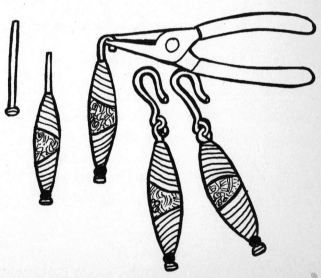

Bugle-bead star earrings

Hang these stars from earrings or a necklace, or use them to decorate a window, gift or tree.

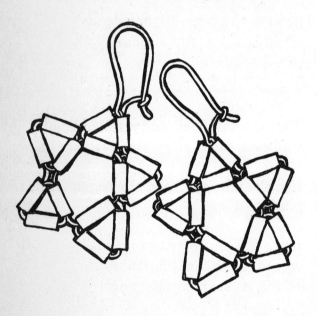

Things you need

- 30 bugle beads, each about 0.5 cm (1/4 in.) long
- 2 pieces of thin beading thread or fishing line, each 60 cm (24 in.) long
- a ruler
- 20 seed beads (optional)
- clear nail polish or white craft glue
- earring wires

1 Thread five bugle beads onto one of the threads. Join them into a pentagon by bringing the thread through the first bugle bead again, from the same direction. Gently slide the pentagon along the thread until it is 15 cm (6 in.) from the left end.

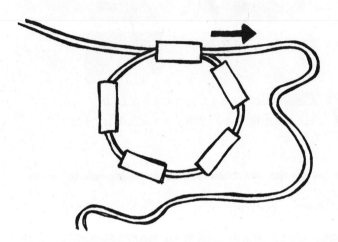

2 Pull the long end of thread through the second bugle bead in the pentagon, beside the one you just came through. Thread two bugle beads onto the long end. Bring the thread through the second bugle bead of the pentagon again to form a triangle.

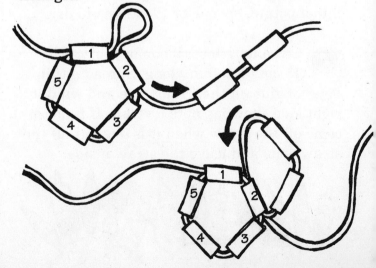

3 Pull the thread through the third pentagon bugle bead, thread on two more beads and go through the third bead again. Continue in this way.

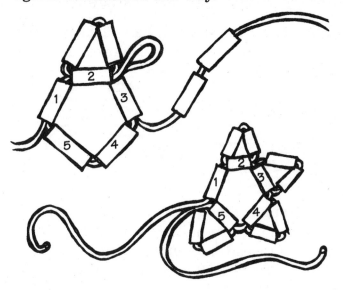

5 Very tightly knot the thread ends at the top of the star. It is optional to thread ten seed beads onto the longer thread end and tie the ends together to form a beaded loop. Weave the thread ends into a couple of bugle beads and then trim them off.

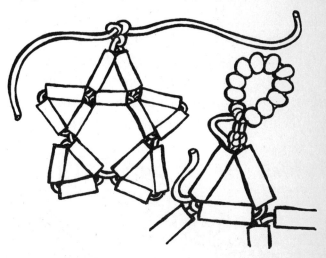

4 When you have made four triangles, bring the thread through the remaining pentagon bugle bead so that a thread hangs out of each end of it. Pull on each end to tighten the star. Thread one bugle bead onto each thread.

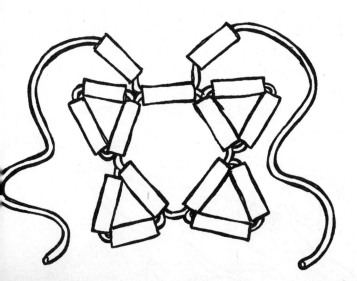

6 Make the other star. If your stars are floppy, put a drop of nail polish (or white craft glue) on each joint. Let them dry and hang them on earring wires.

Macramé bracelet

If you make this bracelet out of jute or hemp thread, it will look thick and earthy. If you use embroidery floss or crochet cotton, it will be fine and thin. Cut longer threads for an anklet.

Things you need

- embroidery floss, crochet cotton or fine jute or hemp thread
- scissors
- a paper clip
- a marker or a small piece of tape

1 Cut a length of floss, cotton or hemp that reaches from your fingertips to your neck. Measure and cut another one about three times as long.

2 Fold each thread in half. Hold the bent ends together and tie an overhand knot, leaving a small loop.

3 Hang the loop on a nail in the wall or on a pin in a bulletin board. Or pull a piece of thread through the loop and tie the threads to a doorknob.

4 Hold the short thread ends together and tie them in an overhand knot as close to the ends as you can. Hook the paper clip onto the handle of the scissors. Open the paper clip slightly so you can hook it onto the short threads above the knotted ends.

5 You should have two short threads weighed down by the scissors with a long thread on each side. Mark the left outside thread by coloring the end with a marker or, if the thread is a dark color, wrap a piece of tape around the end of it.

6 Bend the marked, left thread across the center threads to make an L shape and bring it behind the right thread.

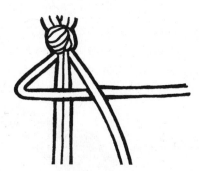

7 Bring the right thread behind the center threads and into the triangle of the L shape on the left side. Pull it through the triangle from behind, so you are pulling it towards you.

8 Gently pull on the left and right threads so they move along the center threads and reach the knot at the top of the bracelet. Lightly tighten the new knot.

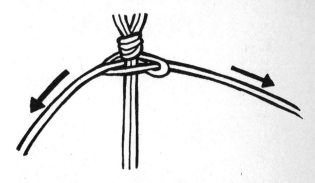

9 Repeat steps 6, 7 and 8, except this time begin by bending the marked thread, this time on the right side, into a backwards L shape.

10 Keep knotting, always starting with the marked thread. It will change sides after each knot. When your bracelet fits around your wrist, remove it from the nail, knot it through the loop end and trim the threads. See page 51 for some variations on this bracelet.

...ramé bead bracelet

Add color to your knotted macramé bracelet by threading on interesting beads.

Things you need

- embroidery floss, crochet cotton or fine jute or hemp thread
- scissors
- a paper clip
- a marker or a small piece of tape
- beads with large holes

---

1 Follow steps 1 to 9 of the Macramé bracelet (see page 48) and make your bracelet about 2.5 cm (1 in.) long.

2 Unhook the paper clip and scissors from the center threads and thread on all the beads you are going to use. If the beads don't fit over the knot, snip off the knot, thread on the beads and knot the threads again. Hook the paper clip and scissors back onto the threads.

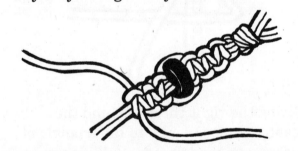

3 Slide a bead up to the knotted part of your bracelet. Make another knot under it, being sure to begin with the marked thread. Continue the bracelet, sliding beads up the center as you need them. It is best to make at least two knots between beads so they stay straight on your bracelet.

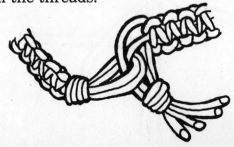

4 If you need more beads, follow step 2 again. When your bracelet fits around your wrist, knot it through the loop end and trim the threads.

Macramé bracelet with a twist

Add some twists and beads for a great-looking bracelet.

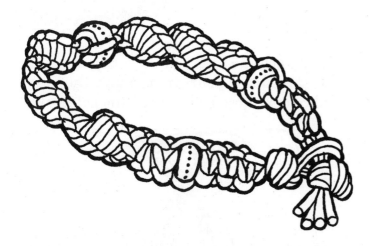

Things you need

- embroidery floss, crochet cotton or fine jute or hemp thread
- scissors
- a paper clip
- a marker or a small piece of tape
- beads with large holes (optional)

1 Follow steps 1 to 8 of the Macramé bracelet (see page 48).

2 Instead of using the marked thread to begin the second knot, use the unmarked one. This means that you will be working on the left side again.

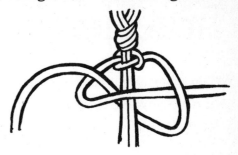

3 Continue on the left side. You will take turns using the marked and the unmarked threads to make the knots. As you go, allow the outside threads to spin and change sides after a few knots. This creates the twist. Keep knotting on the left side.

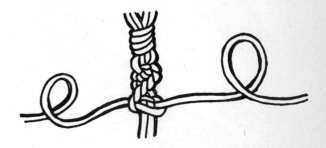

4 Continue with your twisted bracelet until the end, or knot a combination of twists and straight areas. Whenever you want a straight area, simply go back to using the marked thread to start each knot. See page 50 for how to add beads. Finish by tying the ends through the loop and trimming them.

Friendship bracelet

Gather together a few friends and spend an enjoyable afternoon making bracelets for each other.

Things you need

- embroidery floss in 3 colors
- scissors
- a safety pin
- masking tape
- a pen

1 Measure a piece of embroidery floss twice as long as your arm. Use it as a guide to cut the other two colors of floss. Think of your colors as A, B and C.

2 Hold the three threads together and fold them in half. Make an overhand knot near the top to create a small loop.

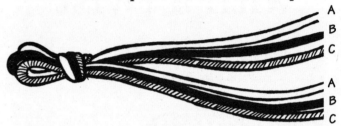

3 Attach the safety pin to a pillow or the knee of your pants. Circle the embroidery floss loop around the safety pin.

4 Separate the threads into the following order: color A, B, C, C, B, A. Stick a small piece of masking tape at the bottom of each thread and label them 1 to 6.

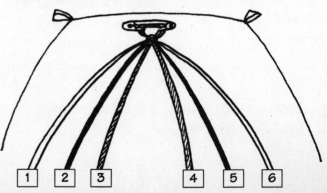

5 Pick up thread 2 in your left hand, and thread 1 in your right hand.

6 Wind thread 1 around thread 2. Holding thread 2, pull forward and up on thread 1 so the loop travels up thread 2 to the overhand knot.

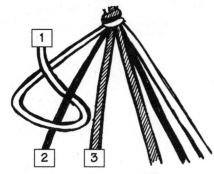

7 Make a second knot around thread 2 to complete the stitch.

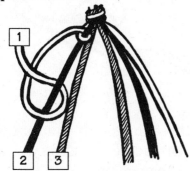

8 Next pick up thread 3 with your left hand and thread 1 again in your right hand. Knot thread 1 around thread 3 twice.

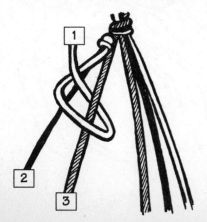

9 Now you will be working on the right side. Pick up thread 5 in your right hand and thread 6 in your left hand. Knot thread 6 around thread 5 twice.

10 Continue with thread 6 by knotting it twice around thread 4 and then around thread 1 in the center.

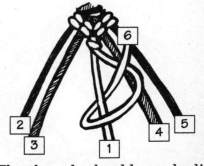

11 The threads should now be lined up as follows: 2, 3, 6, 1, 4, 5. Now you will knot with thread 2 and then thread 5.

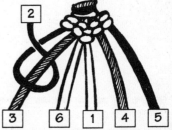

12 When your friendship bracelet fits around your wrist, remove it from the pin, tie the ends through the loop and trim the ends.

Button bracelet

Shank buttons have a looped piece on the back rather than holes right through them. Look for a variety of unusual or antique buttons to make this unique bracelet.

Things you need

- elastic thread
- about 30 shank buttons, assorted colors and sizes
- scissors
- white craft glue or clear nail polish

1 Cut a piece of elastic thread about three times the length around your wrist.

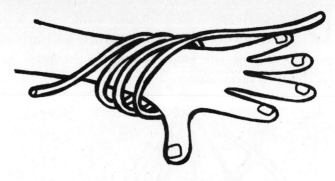

2 Knot a shank button onto one end of the elastic thread. Leave a tail about 5 cm (2 in.) long.

3 Start threading on the buttons. If your elastic thread begins to fray, trim off the end and keep going.

4 When you get close to finishing, try on your bracelet. Add more or remove buttons so your bracelet will fit.

5 Tie the elastic ends together. Triple knot them and trim them. Put a drop of glue or nail polish on the knot to secure it.

⊙ You can make a bracelet out of regular two-hole buttons, too. Follow step 1, then thread the buttons on, good side up, by weaving the elastic in and out of the holes from underneath. Thread on as many buttons as you need. Tie, trim and secure the elastic thread ends. When you put the bracelet on, turn all the buttons good side up so not much elastic shows.

▪▪▪▪▪▪▪▪▪▪▪▪▪▪▪▪▪▪▪▪▪▪▪▪

More ideas

⊙ For a fancy bracelet, use only gold, silver or pearly shank buttons with metallic elastic thread.

Worry-doll pin

This worry-doll pin can be worn on a jacket, hat, sweatshirt or shoes. Or you can leave off the pin and hang it from an earring wire or necklace.

Things you need

- a pipe cleaner
- a ruler
- scissors
- embroidery floss in 2 colors (or variegated floss)
- white craft glue
- small wooden bead
- a small safety pin
- fine, permanent marker

1 Cut a 6-cm (2 ¼-in.) piece and a 10-cm (4-in.) piece from the pipe cleaner.

2 Cut three strands of embroidery floss in one color, each 15 cm (6 in.) long for hair. Tie the strands around the middle of the longer piece of pipe cleaner. Bend the pipe cleaner in half.

3 Dab some glue on the bent end of the pipe cleaner just below the hair. Poke both ends of the pipe cleaner into the bead and slide the bead up to the hair so that no pipe cleaner shows above it.

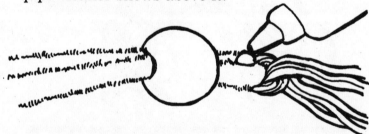

4 Place the short piece of pipe cleaner behind the doubled pipe cleaner so that one side is a little longer than the other. Wrap the long side around the body and return it to the arm position.

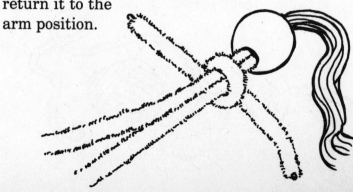

5 Fold over the end of each pipe cleaner to look like hands and feet.

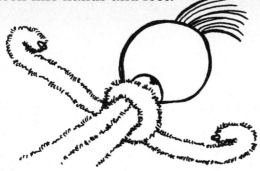

6 Place the end of the other color of floss along one arm. Begin winding the floss around the arm, starting at the wrist. Cover the floss end as you wind.

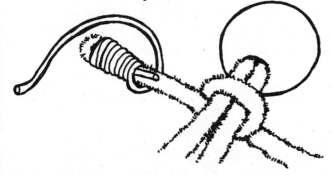

7 Wind the floss across the shoulders to the other wrist and back to the shoulders. Criss-cross around the shoulders and wind down the body. Wind down one leg, up that leg, down the other leg and up until you are back to the waist.

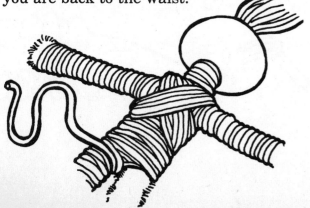

8 Open the safety pin and place it against your doll's back. Wrap the floss around the doll's waist and shoulders several times to hold the pin in place.

9 Dot glue on the back. Cut off the floss and press it into the glue until it begins to dry. Finish your worry doll with a face and a hair style.

More ideas

● To hang the doll from a necklace or earring wire, leave out the glue at step 3. Push the pipe cleaner through the bead so that the bent end sticks out. (You may need to adjust the hair.) Use this looped end to attach onto jewelry.

Hat flowers

These fabric flowers look especially pretty when you have two or three in different colors together on the brim of your hat.

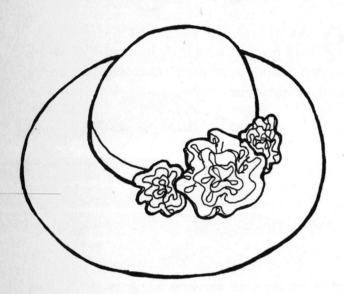

1 Trim off the corners of the fabric strip and fold the strip in half lengthwise, with the wrong sides together. Pin it along the open edges.

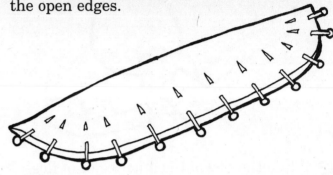

2 Thread two arm lengths of thread into the needle. Double the thread and knot the ends. Make a long running stitch (see page 202) along the unfinished edges of the fabric. Remove the pins as you sew.

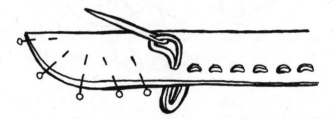

3 If you begin to run out of thread, pull on the thread so that the fabric gathers. When you reach the end, pull some more on the thread and gather the fabric until the strip is about 30 cm (12 in.) long.

Things you need

- a strip of fabric
  6 cm x 90 to 100 cm
  (about 2 1/4 in. x
  3 ft.)
- scissors
- pins
- a needle
- thread to match
  your fabric
- a ruler
- a wide-brimmed
  fabric or straw hat

4 Make a few stitches in one spot on the end of the strip to hold the gathers in place. Do not cut the thread. Spread the gathers evenly along the strip of fabric.

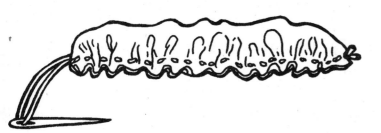

5 Start at the end where you began the running stitch. Roll the gathered fabric so that the unfinished edges are even. Keep rolling until you reach the end where your needle and thread are hanging.

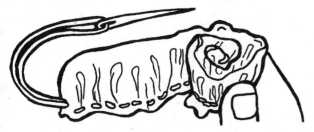

6 Push the needle and thread across the bottom of the flower, going through as many layers as you can. Criss-cross back and forth through the layers until you run out of thread. Finish off by stitching a few times on the same spot before you cut the thread.

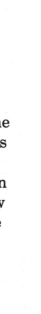

7 Turn the flower over and gently pull the gathers apart. If they are all attached at the bottom, you're finished. If some of the gathers pull up, thread your needle again and do some more stitching.

8 Sew your flower on a fabric hat to hold up the brim at the front, or make two or three to decorate a baseball cap or the brim of a straw hat. If you have a glue gun, have an adult help you hot-glue the flowers in place.

More ideas

Make ribbon roses using a piece of ribbon about 50 cm (20 in.) long. If you use wide ribbon, trim the corners and fold the ribbon in half as you would for the fabric flowers. If you use narrow ribbon, trim only the lower corners on both ends and gather it in a single layer.

Be a mad hatter!

A wide-brimmed fabric or straw hat is great for hiding from the sun and it's perfect for decorating, too.

Ribbons and flowers

Decorate your hat simply for everyday wear, or make it fancy for a special occasion.

● Glue, tie or sew satin ribbons around the brim of your hat. You can leave the ribbon ends hanging down the back or trim them off. Glue or sew dried, silk or plastic flowers on top of the ribbon. For a dressy hat, add strips of craft netting or fine tulle and lace, sequins, gold or silver cord or pearls.

Hatbands

These work especially well on a sturdy hat, such as a felt or a woven straw hat. Any hatband should be glued or sewn down to keep it in place.

● Try threading dozens of beads or shank buttons on heavy, doubled thread or an elastic cord.

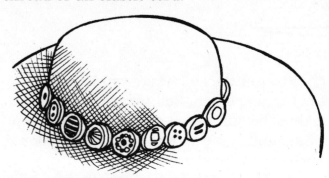

● Make a couple of tassels and matching twisted floss (see page 96) out of embroidery floss. Position the tassels to hang down one side or from the back.

● For a quick hatband, tie a bandanna, scarf or long strip of fabric around your hat.

Hat tricks

These fun decorating ideas work well on a baseball cap or on any hat with a brim. The items can be sewn or glued in place. Make one for yourself or personalize a hat for a friend.

● Make a fishing hat by sewing or gluing on plastic fish, sinkers, bobbers, rubber worms and other fishing tackle (without hooks).

● A gardening hat could have flowers, mini tools, fake fruit and vegetables, empty seed packets, and plastic ladybugs and butterflies for decoration.

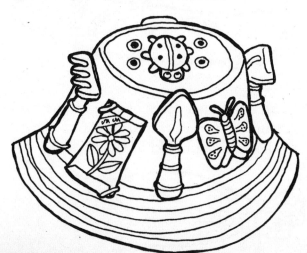

● For a bird-watching hat, attach artificial birds, twigs, feathers, mini binoculars, or a pencil and small checklist of rare birds.

● Just for fun, how about attaching huge roly eyes to the front of a hat? Or sewing on plastic spiders, lizards and snakes? Or how about a few big splatters of white paint on a hat with the words "Darn pigeons!"?

Hair band

This is a great way to give an old hair band new life. Look for fabric to match your clothes or try a colorful bandanna.

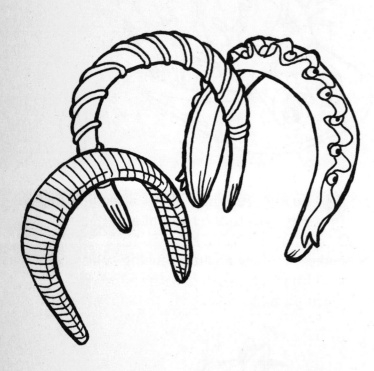

Things you need

- a hair band — plain or fabric covered
- a ruler or a measuring tape
- fabric
- scissors
- pins
- a needle and thread
- a knitting needle or a new unsharpened pencil

1 Measure the length of your hair band from one tip around to the other tip.

2 Cut or tear a piece of fabric that is 5 cm (2 in.) longer than the hair band. If the hair band is narrow, the width of the fabric should be about 5 cm (2 in.). If the hair band is a regular width, the fabric should be about 8 cm (3 in.) wide.

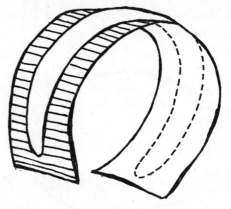

3 Pin the good sides of the fabric together along the entire length. Backstitch (see page 202) this length (or sew by machine).

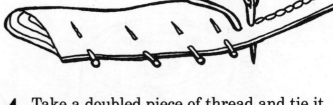

4 Take a doubled piece of thread and tie it as tightly as you can around one short end to close it. Double knot the thread.

5 Use the knitting needle or the pencil to turn the fabric right side out.

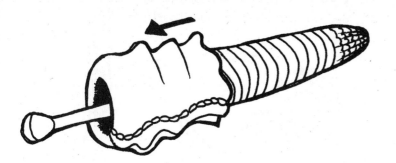

6 Push one end of the hair band into the open end of the fabric cover.

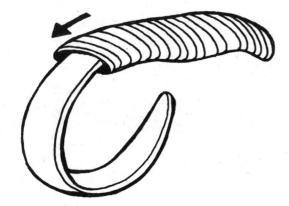

7 When the hair band reaches the closed end, arrange the fabric so that the seam is on the underside of the hair band.

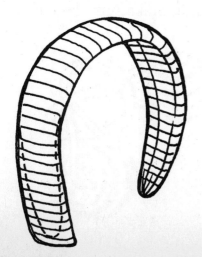

8 Tuck in the edges of the fabric on the open end. Sew this end closed.

More ideas

Dress up a plain hair band by decorating it with fabric paint. Try criss-crossing narrow ribbon or flat lace from one tip to the other. Try tying, sewing or gluing on silk or dried flowers. You could also glue on rhinestones or beads.

Ponytail holder

A ponytail holder can be worn to jazz up ponytails, braids and other hair styles.

1 Cut a piece of elastic about 30 cm (12 in.) long.

2 Thread both large beads onto it. Tie the elastic ends in an overhand knot.

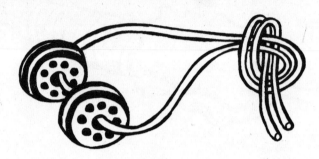

3 Pull the beads apart from each other. Position the knot in the center between them. If the hole in one of your beads is large enough, tuck the knot inside it instead.

4 Pinch together the center areas of the elastic cord and tie a loose knot. Before you tighten it, make sure the knot is centered.

Things you need

- strong, round elastic cord
- a ruler
- scissors
- 2 large beads

5 To wear this ponytail holder, hold one bead on top of the ponytail as you wrap the other one around. Slide the wrap-around bead over the other one. If this isn't tight enough, wrap it around twice.

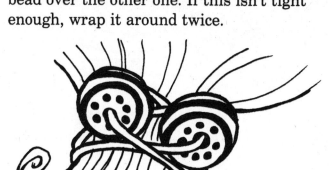

Cut a length of elastic cord about 20 cm (8 in.) long. Thread on interesting shank buttons or beads until there is only enough elastic left to make a knot. Wrap this accessory around a ponytail.

▪▫▪▫▪▫▪▫▪▫▪▫▪▫▪▫▪▫▪▫▪▫▪▫▪▫

More ideas

Instead of using two large beads, use two large, fancy shank buttons or several smaller shank buttons. Or make two special beads out of modeling clay such as Fimo.

Cut a length of leather lacing at least 50 cm (20 in.) long. Thread a few beads on one end. Knot the leather so that the beads can't fall off. Thread a few beads on the other end and knot it, too. Tie this over a covered elastic on a ponytail.

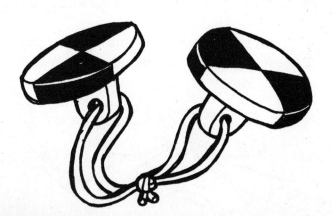

Barrette bow

This is a quick and easy way to change a barrette from plain to pretty.

Things you need

- a plain barrette
- a piece of ribbon 50 cm (20 in.) long
- white craft glue
- scissors
- clear nail polish (optional)

1 Slip the ribbon through the barrette and center it.

2 Make a loop in the ribbon on each side of the barrette. Cross one loop over the other and tie it.

3 Adjust the bow so it is smooth and even on the barrette. Lightly glue it in place.

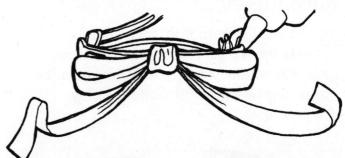

4 Trim the ribbon ends and apply a thin coat of glue or nail polish to keep them from fraying.

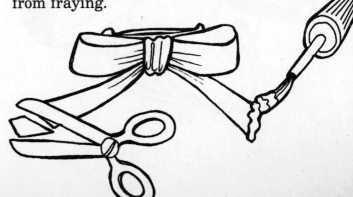

More barrette bows

Try barrettes with different sizes and colors of ribbon for a whole new look.

1 Fold one piece of ribbon so that the ends overlap. Place it on the barrette.

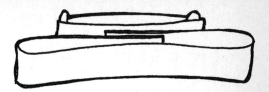

2 Slip the other piece of ribbon through the barrette and tie it around the folded ribbon.

3 Slide the knot under the barrette and glue the bow in place.

4 Trim the ribbon ends and apply a thin coat of glue or nail polish to keep them from fraying.

Things you need

- 2 different-colored pieces of ribbon, each at least 20 cm (8 in.) long
- a plain barrette
- white craft glue
- scissors
- clear nail polish (optional)

More ideas

Use two or three different colors and widths of ribbon folded one on top of the other, or use different colors and widths of ribbon to tie the bow. You could also tie the folded ribbons with gold or silver cord, thick rickrack, craft netting or a combination of materials.

Splashy scrunchee

Scrunchees can hold hair styles such as ponytails or buns. Make them out of many different fabrics so you have some for everyday as well as for special occasions. Make a few extra scrunchees to give as gifts.

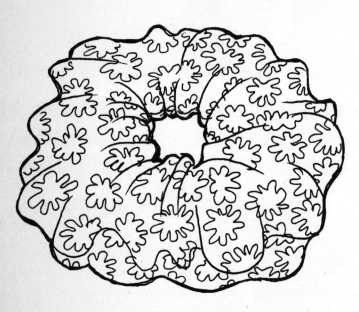

Things you need

- fabric
- scissors
- pins
- a needle and thread
- a safety pin
- elastic 0.5 cm (1/4 in.) wide
- sticky tape

1 Cut or tear a piece of fabric 10 cm x 55 cm (4 in. x 22 in.).

2 Fold and pin it in half lengthwise, with the good sides together.

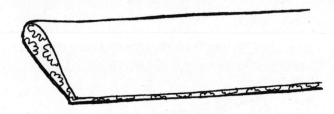

3 Backstitch a seam (see page 202) along this pinned side, or sew it by machine. This seam should be about 1 cm (1/2 in.) in from the pinned side. Remove the pins as you sew.

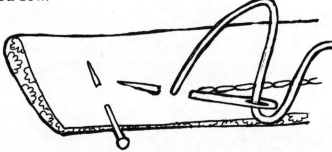

4 Fasten the safety pin to the seam area of one end. Tuck it into the fabric tube and weave it through to the other end to turn the fabric right side out.

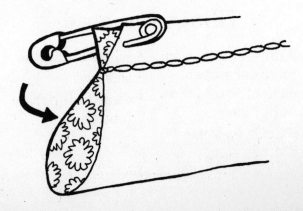

5 Cut a 23-cm (9-in.) length of elastic. Tape one end to your work table and fasten the safety pin to the other end. Thread the elastic through the tube using the pin.

6 Remove the tape from the elastic. Overlap the ends of the elastic and use the needle with double thread to sew them together.

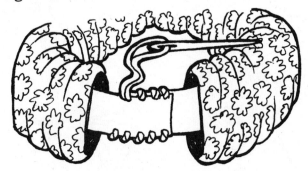

7 Tuck one end of the tube into the other and try to match the seam. Fold under the unfinished edge of the fabric on top.

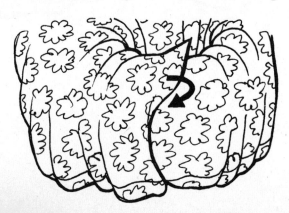

8 Stitch the folded edge to the tucked-in edge, all the way around.

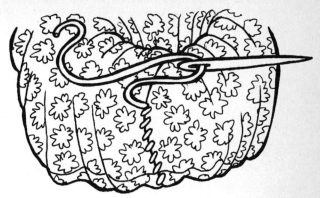

More ideas

● You can make four mini-scrunchees out of the fabric needed for one regular scrunchee. Cut the fabric 5 cm x 28 cm (2 in. x 11 in.). Use a piece of elastic 15 cm (6 in.) long.

● Make a scrunchee hair band. Cut the fabric 7.5 cm x 65 cm (3 in. x 25 in.). Measure your head and use that measurement to cut the elastic, likely about 50 cm (20 in.) long.

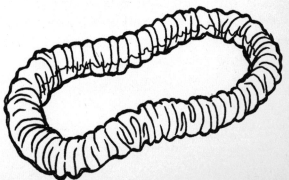

Tie-dye T-shirt

One of the best things about tie-dyeing T-shirts is that each shirt is a one-of-a-kind work of art. Be sure to cover your work surface before you start, and wear an old shirt and rubber gloves.

Things you need

- a 100% cotton white or light-colored T-shirt
- rubber bands in various widths
- an old pail or dishpan
- a glass or plastic bowl or large jar
- cold-water dye and cold dye fix (available at craft and hobby stores)
- an old spoon
- table salt
- clean rags

1 Your T-shirt should be clean and wet, but not dripping wet. If it is new, wash it, but don't dry it.

2 Use rubber bands to fasten large and small bundles of fabric all over the front and back of your T-shirt. Fasten each bundle with one or more different-sized rubber bands to create lines of various widths.

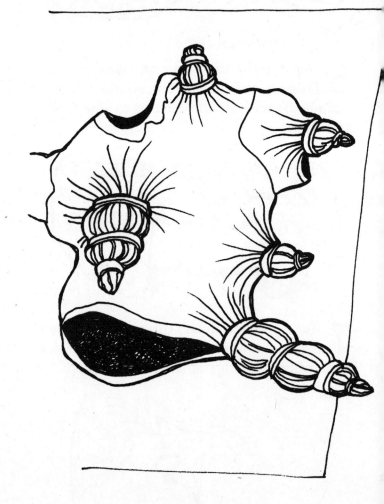

3 Pour 1½ to 2 L (6 to 8 c.) of cold water into your pail. Place the dyeing pail in a sink or laundry tub so any spills go down the drain.

4 Pour 500 mL (2 c.) of hot tap water into your glass or plastic bowl.

5 Carefully open the dye package according to the manufacturer's instructions. If it is powder, do not breathe it in. Pour it into the hot water and stir it. Pour this dye mixture into the cold-water pail. Rinse out the bowl.

6 Pour 500 mL (2 c.) of hot tap water again into the glass or plastic bowl. Pour in the cold dye fix. Add about 75 mL (6 tbsp.) of table salt. Stir until it is dissolved. Pour this mixture into the dyeing pail, too. Stir the dye and fix mixture thoroughly.

7 Place the tied T-shirt in the dye. Slowly stir and gently push down the shirt for about 10 minutes. Let it sit for another 50 minutes, stirring it now and then.

8 Remove the T-shirt from the pail. Rinse it thoroughly under cold running water until the water runs almost clear. Squeeze out as much water as possible and roll it in clean rags to remove extra water.

9 Remove all the rubber bands. Wash and dry your T-shirt separately before you wear it.

More tie-dye

There's no right or wrong way to tie your T-shirt. Here are some interesting ties to try using the dyeing instructions on page 70.

Spiral design

Place your wet T-shirt front side down. Pinch some fabric in the center. Turn your hand so that the fabric starts to swirl around the center. Pull at the outer edges as you go so that the folds stay neat. When it's in a tight disk, stretch three or four rubber bands around it. Don't worry if it gets a little squashed or the center pops up. Dye it as usual.

Folds

Place your wet T-shirt flat on your work surface. Fanfold the shirt from top to bottom, side to side or on a diagonal. Use rubber bands or strong household string to hold the folds, then dye it.

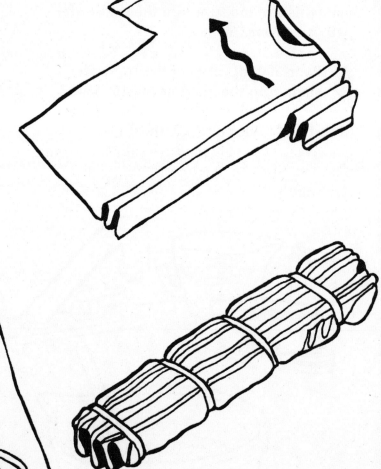

More-than-one-color dyeing

If you'd like to try different colors, always begin with the lightest one. Tie and dye your T-shirt. Remove the rubber bands and make sure the shirt is rinsed free of extra dye. Squeeze out as much extra water as you can and begin again with another color.

More to tie than Ts

For small items such as socks, shoelaces, hankies and undies, you can tie and dye one or two of them using the leftover dye mixture from your T-shirt. The colors won't be as bold, but it's a good way to get the most from your dyes. This works best with dark dye colors. Make sure that the items you are dyeing are made from a natural fiber such as cotton.

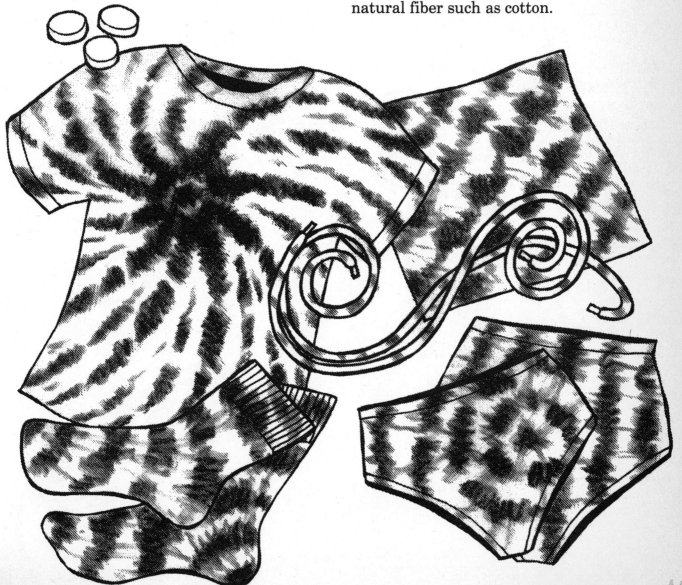

73

Wearable art

Did you know you can print just about anything you can wear? Choose a decorating method from the following pages and get printing!

Things you need

- an article of clothing such as a T-shirt, sweatshirt, shorts, running shoes or hat
- a paint shirt or old clothes
- fabric paint
- scrap paper
- printing supplies (see pages 76–77)

1 Your article of clothing should be washed, dry and smooth for printing. You don't need to wash shoes or laces, and wash your hat only if it is washable and likely to be washed often.

2 Cover your work surface and your own clothes. Here's how to prepare different articles of clothing for printing.

- Put cardboard in between the two layers of fabric for a shirt, shorts, jacket or socks.

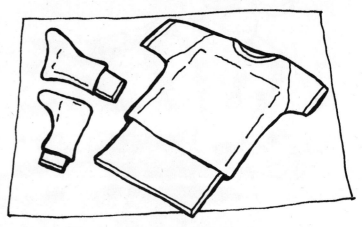

- Remove the laces from shoes and fill the toes with crumpled scrap paper.

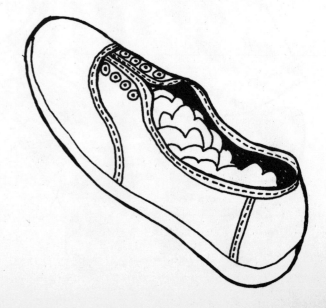

• Tape the ends of shoelaces to your work surface.

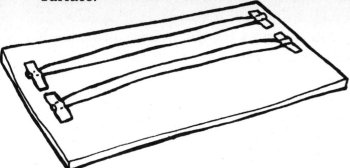

• Stuff a hat with crumpled paper or place it over an upside-down bowl.

3 Use one of the ideas on the following pages to print your clothing. For some of these ideas you will need to pour small amounts of fabric paint into shallow containers such as foil pie plates. Test your designs on scrap paper first. If you are printing on non-white fabric, test your paint colors by dabbing a spot of paint on an inside hem or seam.

4 When your article of clothing is dry, you need to set the paint. Cover the painted area with a clean cloth and iron it on a hot setting for two minutes (unless the manufacturer gives different instructions). Shoes can be placed in a hot dryer for a few minutes.

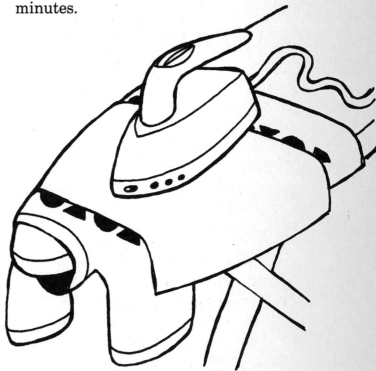

Plenty of printing possibilities

Here are lots of ideas to help you leave your creative mark on your clothes. Use the printing instructions on page 74.

Flower power

Slice a potato in half. Draw a simple flower shape on scrap paper. Cut it out and place it on the wet, cut surface of the potato. Cut into the potato around the flower. Cut out the center of the potato flower, too. Repeatedly dip the flower into the fabric paint and print all over the front of your shirt. Cut a small circle into another piece of potato or slice a carrot in half. Use a different-colored paint to print a circle in the center of each flower.

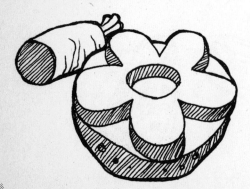

Potato printing

Experiment with different designs cut into a potato. Try geometric shapes, stars, faces, hearts, animals, bugs, birds and so on. If you want to use the same potato shape with another paint color, rinse and dry it before using the new color. You can print all over your item of clothing, just around the yoke of a shirt, on a pocket, in the center or wherever you like.

Drizzle and splatter

Dip a Popsicle stick into paint and let it drizzle and drip onto the fabric. Or dip the bristles of an old toothbrush into paint and, holding the bristles downward, flick them with a Popsicle stick. Use many colors. You can use these methods with a stencil, too.

Handprints and footprints

Use your hands to decorate your clothes. You can print with your knuckles, open hand or the little-finger side of your fist for a hand-footprint. Make toes by dipping your fingertips into paint. Also, apply fabric paint to the bottom of an old pair of running shoes and "walk" them across your clothes.

More printing possibilities

Dip any of the following items into paint on a shallow tray and print with them: cut vegetables, sponge shapes, pipe cleaners bent into designs or string glued onto a small block of wood.

Print on fabric grocery, book or lunch bags or on cloth napkins, placemats or tablecloths. For your bedroom, print a pillow, chair pad or plain window dressing.

Have a printing party. Invite your friends to bring a T-shirt and fabric paint. Share ideas or print and sign an area of one another's shirts.

Gifts to make

Warm someone's heart with a handcrafted gift. Make a fancy bookmark with colorful tassels, paint a clay pot, create a unique papier-mâché bowl or a potpourri pomander. Brighten someone's day with a beeswax or striped candle. Decorate a personalized lunch bag to make a friend's lunchtime a real treat. Not only are there plenty of gift ideas here, there are great ideas for wrapping them up, too. You'll find that it's as much fun to make gift boxes and wrapping paper as it is to make the gifts inside.

Papier-mâché bowl

You'll be amazed when you see that you can make a bowl out of newspaper, flour, salt and water. Papier mâché shouldn't be rushed, so cover a table with a garbage bag and leave this work area set up for a few days.

Things you need

- a ruler
- newspaper
- a bowl to use as a mold — a large, smooth one without a rim is best
- plastic cling-wrap
- masking tape
- a mixing bowl
- flour
- salt
- a fork
- fine sandpaper
- gesso for undercoating and sealing (available at craft and hobby stores)
- acrylic paints, varnish and a paintbrush

1 Using the edge of the ruler as a guide, tear six large sheets of newspaper into strips about 3 cm x 30 cm (1 in. x 12 in.).

2 Cover the outside of the mold bowl with plastic wrap. Make sure you don't poke any holes in it and make it as smooth as possible. Tape the plastic to the inside of the bowl.

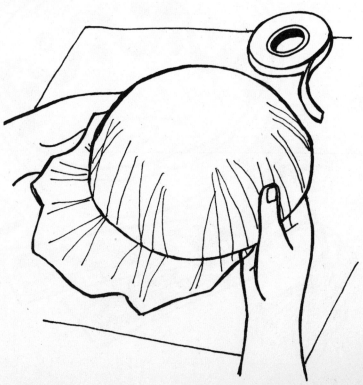

3 To make papier-mâché paste, mix together 175 mL (¾ c.) of flour, 30 mL (2 tbsp.) of salt and 350 mL (1½ c.) of water in the mixing bowl. Use a fork and your fingers to get out all the lumps.

4 Dip a newspaper strip into the paste. As you take it out, run it between your fingers to get off the extra paste. Smooth the strip onto the bowl.

5 Apply one or two layers at a time, placing the strips of each layer in the opposite direction to the layer before. Make small tears in the strips or tear them into smaller pieces so they lie flat. Smooth them with your fingers to get out bubbles and raised areas. Dab the strips with a cloth if they get too wet.

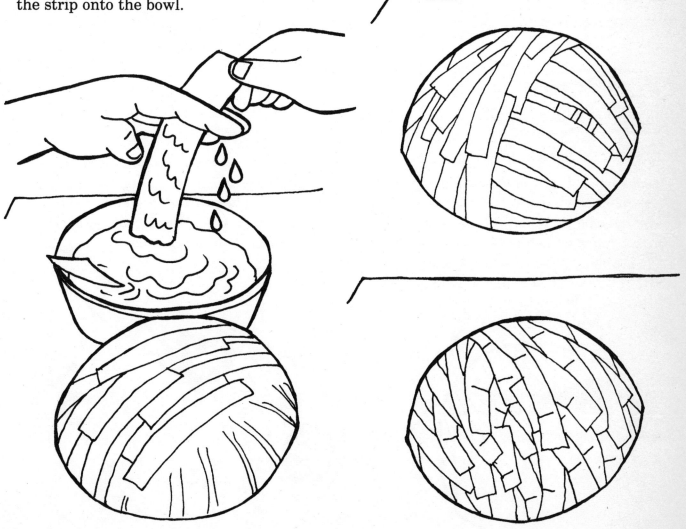

Continued on next page

6 Depending on the drying conditions, it will take between 10 and 24 hours for the papier mâché to be dry enough for another layer. If your work area is not very warm, you can move your bowl near a heat register or outside on a warm, dry day. Cover and refrigerate the papier-mâché paste between sessions.

7 Apply between 8 and 16 layers of newspaper. Eight layers will give you a thin, flexible bowl, while 16 will give you a sturdy, thick bowl. When you have enough layers on your bowl and it feels dry, remove it from the mold bowl. If you have any difficulty, it may need to dry a little longer. Or it may be a little stuck, so use a dull knife to pry it off.

8 Before finishing your bowl, you may want to sand it to remove paste and other bumps. Wipe it thoroughly and then apply a coat of gesso inside and outside. Apply another coat if the first one hasn't completely covered the print on the newspaper.

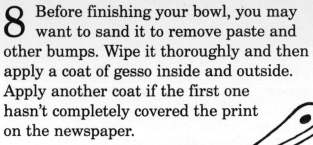

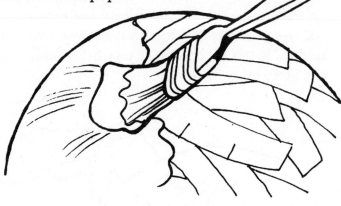

9 Decorate your bowl, using découpage (see page 10) or stenciling (see page 182). Or simply paint on a scene or sponge-print it. Apply at least two coats of acrylic varnish over your decorating.

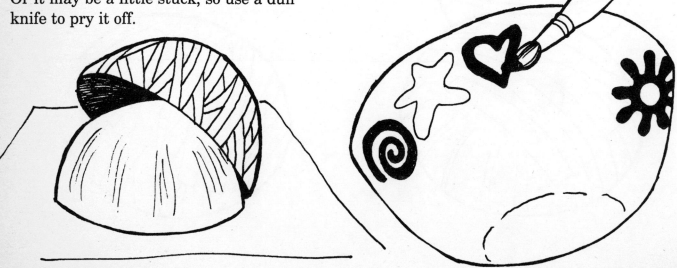

10 This bowl should not be immersed in water. However, it can be used to hold snacks (line it with a napkin first), wrapped candies or potpourri. You can give it a quick wipe with a damp cloth to clean it.

More ideas

Make a papier-mâché vase out of a jar or bottle. The pasted strips should go all around the sides and bottom and slightly over the top edge to the inside of the jar. Be sure to coat the finished vase with acrylic varnish. If you use it to hold fresh flowers, don't fill the jar quite full to the top with water. This vase would also look lovely with dried or silk flowers in it.

Papier-mâché napkin rings

Make these to match a papier-mâché bowl or make them a completely different design.

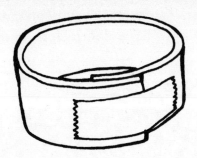

2 Dip a strip of newspaper into the paste. Run it between your fingers to get off the extra paste.

3 Wrap it around a cardboard circle, overlapping as you go.

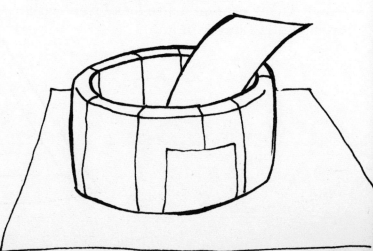

Things you need

- a strip of thin cardboard 2 cm x 20 cm (³/₄ in. x 8 in.) for each napkin ring
- masking tape
- narrow strips of newspaper
- papier-mâché paste (see page 80)
- fine sandpaper
- gesso (available at craft and hobby stores)
- a paintbrush

4 Keep wrapping strips until you've covered all the cardboard rings. Allow the rings to dry and apply another layer or two. Finish each with a strip smoothed all around the outside.

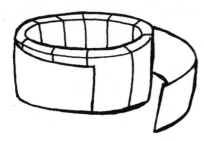

5 When they are completely dry, sand the napkin rings to remove extra paste and other bumps. Wipe them and apply a coat or two of gesso to each one.

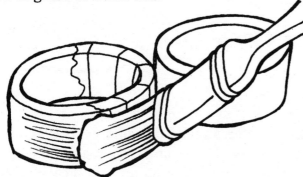

6 See step 9 on page 82 for decorating ideas.

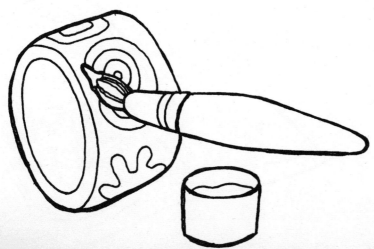

See step 9 on page 82 for decorating ideas.

More ideas

Make a bangle for your wrist. Use a strip of thin cardboard from 1 to 4 cm (¹/₂ to 1¹/₂ in.) wide and 20 to 25 cm (8 to 10 in.) long. When it is taped in a circle it should slide loosely over your hand. (The opening of the circle will be a little smaller when you are finished with the papier mâché.) Decorate it with paint, sequins or rhinestones.

Pressed flowers

When you press flowers, you preserve their natural color and beauty for years. The most suitable flowers are brightly colored and not too thick. Leaves from trees, shrubs, weeds and vines all press well, too. Always get permission to pick flowers.

1 Pick or cut the flowers on a dry day so they are not damp. Pick only as many as you can press at a time so they don't wilt.

2 Open the phone book near the back. Place a few flowers and leaves face down on the page. Make sure that the flowers are as open and flat as possible. Leave lots of space around each one.

3 If you are using newspaper and a catalog instead of a phone book, place at least two layers of newspaper in the open catalog. Lay the plants on it and carefully place two layers of newspaper on top.

Things you need

- an assortment of fresh flowers and leaves
- an old phone book, or newspaper and a catalog
- scrap paper and a pencil
- heavy books

4 Write the date on a scrap of paper and use it to mark the page.

5 Gently roll some of the phone book or catalog pages closed over the plants. Place more plants in the book for pressing, marking the pages.

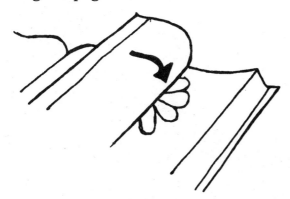

6 Lay the book or catalog flat in a warm, dry place where it is not likely to be disturbed. Place a few heavy books on top.

7 Wait at least one week before you check the plants. If they are stuck to the paper or feel damp, they are not ready. Check them again in a week.

8 Remove some to make crafts and press more. Keep adding to your collection. Pressed flowers can be stored in a book for months or years. Turn to page 130 to see how to make a greeting card. You can use this same method to make a bookmark or gift tag.

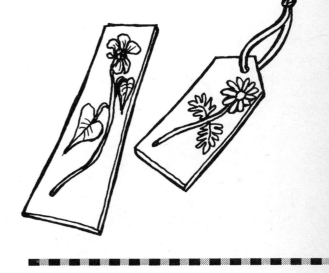

More ideas

Since thick flowers like roses do not press well, you can remove the petals and leaves and press them separately. Use them as you would use other pressed plants.

Drying flowers

Use fresh, healthy-looking flowers for drying. Cut them on a dry day just before they are in full bloom. Ask for permission to pick flowers. Use dried flowers in bouquets, for decorating wreaths and baskets and for making potpourri.

Things you need

- an assortment of fresh flowers, weeds and grasses, with stems but not roots
- scissors
- rubber bands
- paper clips
- gardening gloves (if you are working with roses)

1 Find a place where you can hang up bunches of flowers for a few weeks. It should be a warm, dry area away from direct sunlight, such as a well-ventilated attic, garage, shed, closet (leave the door slightly open so the air can circulate) or the rafters in a furnace room. If none of these are possible for you, hang them wherever you can, even from a nail on the wall.

2 Use a rubber band to bundle a few flowers together at the stems. Position the flowers at different levels so their heads do not touch. Hang large flowers by themselves.

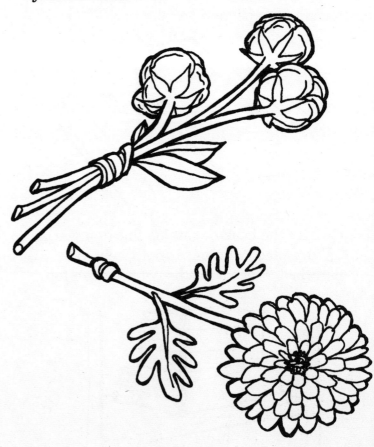

3 Open a paper clip so it has a hook on each end. Hook one end into the rubber band. Use the other end to hang the bundle of flowers upside down.

4 The amount of drying time will depend on the size and thickness of the flowers as well as the weather. They will likely take at least two weeks to dry, and as long as a month.

5 When the flowers are dry, arrange them in a vase, use them on a wreath (see page 150), or display them in a decorated basket (see page 112) or twig basket (see page 144). They also look great hanging in bundles in a kitchen.

More ideas

Large flowers such as peonies or flat ones such as Queen Anne's lace can be dried on a cookie rack or an old piece of screen with holes poked into it. Drop the stems through the rack so the flower heads rest on it. Suspend the rack between two chairs or two piles of books.

You can also dry flower petals and leaves. They will dry quicker when they're off the stem. Pull them off a fresh flower and place them in a single layer on a newspaper-lined plate or tray or on a screen. Turn them over often. See page 90 for how to use them in potpourri.

Making potpourri

Potpourri is a fragrant mixture of dried flowers, petals, leaves and whatever else you'd like to include in it. You can dry the plants yourself (see page 88) or you can buy them already dried from a florist or a craft supply store.

Things you need

- a variety of dried plants, such as roses, lavender, statice, Queen Anne's lace and hydrangeas
- a mixing bowl
- a small paper or plastic bag (optional)
- fragrant potpourri oil, herbs or spices (optional)
- a container with a lid

1 Gently pull the petals and leaves off the stems and into the mixing bowl. If the plants have small flowers, pull them off the stems whole. Seed pods can be used whole, too.

2 Stir the mixture with your hands. Add more color or variety if it needs it.

3 Smell the potpourri. If you like the fragrance, your potpourri is ready. If it needs a stronger smell, read on.

4 Place the mixture in the paper bag. Add one or two drops of fragrant oil, or a spoonful of crumbled herbs such as basil or rosemary or a spice such as whole cloves or ground cinnamon.

5 Close the bag and shake it gently. Smell the mixture again and add more fragrance if it needs it.

6 Empty the potpourri into a container with a lid. Open it when you want to fill the room with the fragrance of the potpourri. Whenever the fragrance fades, you can freshen it by adding more fragrant oil or spice.

More ideas

● You can add dried lemon and orange peel to the potpourri. To dry peel, slice it thinly and place it on a plate in a warm place for a few days. Or try tossing in a cinnamon stick or two.

● The potpourri should look as good as it smells. When you've emptied it into a container, top off the mixture with a couple of whole dried flowers such as roses or colorful straw flowers.

● Potpourri can also be displayed in an open bowl, perhaps one you make yourself out of papier mâché (see page 80).

Potpourri pomander

A pomander is a sweet-smelling, decorative ball. It makes a lovely gift to show off your homemade potpourri. But, store-bought potpourri works well, too.

Things you need

- a paper clip
- a medium-sized Styrofoam ball (available at craft stores)
- potpourri (see page 90)
- a plate
- white craft glue
- ribbon

1 Unbend the paper clip so that one end is straight and the other is a hook.

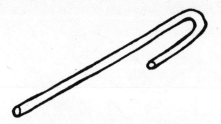

2 Poke it into the Styrofoam ball so that the top of the hook is sticking out. You may need to use wire-cutters to cut off the straight end of the paper clip if it sticks out the other side of the ball.

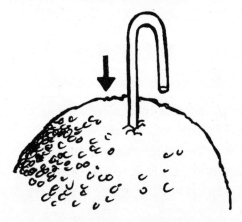

3 Scoop some potpourri onto the plate. Crush or tear some of it in your fingers so there is a variety of sizes.

4 Hold the Styrofoam ball by the hook and spread glue on part of it.

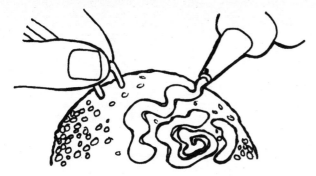

5 Holding the ball by the hook, slowly and firmly roll the glue area around in the potpourri. Leave the ball on the potpourri plate and let it dry for a couple of hours.

6 Gradually apply glue and potpourri to the rest of the ball. It may take a while to cover it completely.

7 Tie a long ribbon onto the paper-clip hook if you want the pomander to be hung up. Otherwise, tie a short piece of ribbon into a bow on the hook.

More ideas

⬤ If the pomander is to be hung up, you can use a straight pin to hang ribbons from the bottom.

⬤ Make a potpourri sachet. Place a small scoop of potpourri in the center of a doily or a circle of craft netting. Tie it with a ribbon. If the potpourri has spice in it that may fall out through the holes in the doily or netting, use a circle of cotton fabric instead.

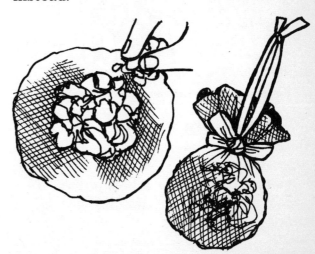

Bookmarks a-plenty

There are many ways to make a bookmark. Check the index in this book for ideas like printing, découpage, stenciling and pressed flowers. Or try this simple bookmark, then turn the page to find out how to make tassels for it.

Things you need

- scraps of wrapping paper
- scissors
- white craft glue
- self-adhesive vinyl
- a hole punch (optional)

1 Cut out a bookmark-size long rectangle from a piece of wrapping paper.

2 Fold it in half lengthwise. Make short cuts from the folded edge to the open side, without cutting through the open side. The cuts can be of various widths and wavy, curved or angled.

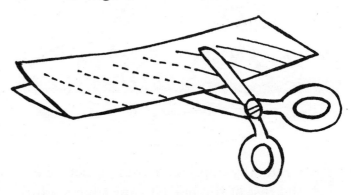

3 Cut three or four narrow strips of another wrapping paper the same length as the long rectangle.

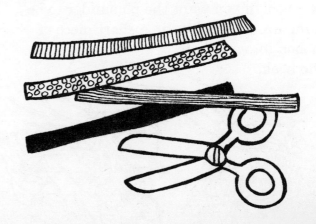

4 Open the rectangle. Start weaving a paper strip down the length of the bookmark through the cuts until you reach the other end. Weave the next strip opposite to the first strip.

6 Cover both sides with vinyl so the bookmark will last a long time.

5 When you are finished weaving strips, glue the strip ends down on the front and back of the bookmark.

7 If you are going to add tassels to your bookmark (see page 96), punch a hole at the top of it. Fold the twisted floss in half and bring the loop through the hole in the bookmark. Bring the tassels through the loop and pull them into position.

Tassels

These colorful tassels look terrific on a hatband or handmade bookmark. They also look great tied around a gift or hanging on a doorknob, blind, drawer knob or anywhere else that needs a splash of color.

Things you need

- embroidery floss in 2 colors
- a ruler
- scissors
- tape

- a sturdy piece of cardboard about 10 cm x 15 cm (4 in. x 6 in.)
- a darning needle (a needle with a large eye)

1 Cut four pieces of floss, two in each color, each about 90 cm (36 in.) long for a hatband and 35 cm (14 in.) long for a bookmark. Hold the four pieces of floss together evenly and overhand knot them at one end. Tape the knot to your work surface.

2 Divide the floss in pairs so that strands of the same color are together. Twist one pair tightly together. Ask someone to hold it taut for you (or hold it in your teeth) while you twist the other pair in the same direction.

3 When both pairs are twisted, keep them taut and overhand knot them together. Release the knot that is taped down and let the floss twist together. Pull on the knotted ends to help the floss twist evenly. Trim the ends.

4 Wind one color of floss around the length of the cardboard about 15 times. Slide it off and cut the loops at both ends. Lay down the bundle of floss.

5 Take one end of the twisted floss and place it on the strands of floss so that the knot is a little past the center point. Tuck the twisted-floss knot among the strands of floss so it is hidden.

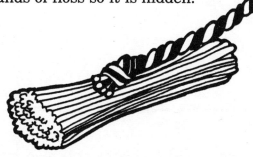

6 Cut a piece of floss (the same color as the bundle of floss) about 30 cm (12 in.) long. Tightly knot it around the center of the bundle of floss, including around the twisted-floss knot.

7 Pick up the twisted floss. Shake the bundle and smooth the strands of floss until you have a tassel shape. The twisted floss should be coming out of the center of the tassel, and the knot should be covered by strands of floss.

8 Cut a 50-cm (20-in.) piece of floss in the other color. Tightly wind it near the top of the tassel, covering the end as you go. Thread the leftover floss into the needle and poke the needle down through the wound area and into the center of the tassel. Trim off the piece of floss.

9 Shake the tassel and trim the uneven ends. Make a tassel on the other end of the length of twisted floss the same way. If the strands of floss are kinked, wet them, squeeze with a cloth and hang to dry.

Bath mitt

Make one of these out of a good section of an old bath towel or buy terry cloth from a fabric store. It makes a nice gift with some soap or bubble bath. You can use a sewing machine or check page 202 for how to hand stitch.

Things you need

- terry cloth
- a ruler or a measuring tape
- scissors
- pins
- a needle and thread
- embroidery floss (optional)

1 Cut a piece of terry cloth about 18 cm x 38 cm (7 in. x 15 in.).

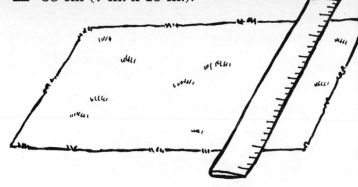

2 With the good side of the cloth down, fold one short side over once and then once again. Pin this narrow hem in place. Do the same for the other short side.

3 Thread two arm lengths of thread into the needle. Double the thread and knot the ends. Flip the cloth over and backstitch along the pinned sides. Remove the pins. Knot and trim the thread ends.

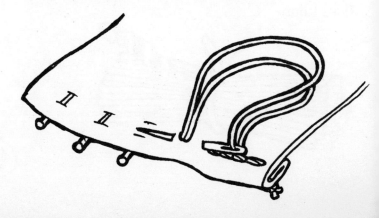

4 Fold the cloth in half with the good sides together. Pin the side seams together. Thread your needle again. Double and knot the thread.

5 Poke the needle into the cloth from underneath about 0.5 cm (¼ in.) from the hemmed end and 1 cm (½ in.) from the side edge. Bring the needle around the end and poke it in about 0.5 cm (¼ in.) to the left of where you first went in, again from underneath.

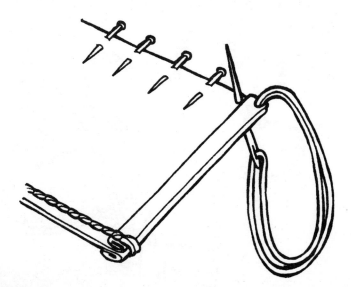

6 Backstitch the side seam, removing the pins as you go. As you finish, make a couple of small stitches in the same spot, knot the thread and trim it. Stitch the other side seam.

7 To prevent the side seams from fraying, overcast stitch them as shown. Finish by making small stitches in one spot, knot the thread and trim it.

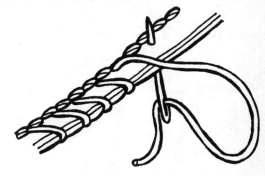

8 Turn the bath mitt right side out. For a finishing touch you can add some embroidery along the hemmed edge (see page 202).

Stuffed felt decorations

Here's a gift to decorate a baby's or a small child's room. Keep in mind that it is not a toy — if you want a young child to be able to handle it, don't put on any beads, ribbon or other small removable parts.

Things you need

- cookie cutters or thin cardboard
- felt
- fabric chalk, fabric marker, or permanent marker
- scissors
- straight pins
- an embroidery needle
- embroidery floss
- polyester fiber stuffing or cotton balls or tissue

1 Trace a cookie cutter shape twice onto felt. If you don't have suitable cookie cutters, you can cut out a simple shape from thin cardboard and trace it twice.

2 Cut out the shapes inside the lines so you don't have any fabric marker on your shape.

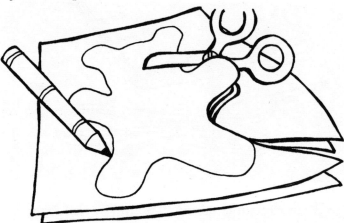

3 Pin the two shapes together all around. Use the blanket stitch as shown to sew most of the way around your shape. Remove the pins as you sew.

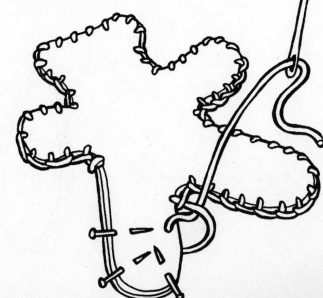

4 Stuff the shape a little and finish it by stitching it closed.

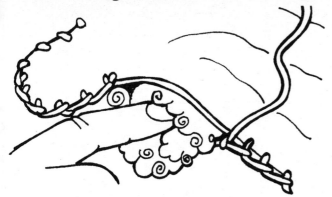

5 If your shape needs a face or other features, embroider them on (see page 202). This can also be done before you pin and stitch the two shapes together.

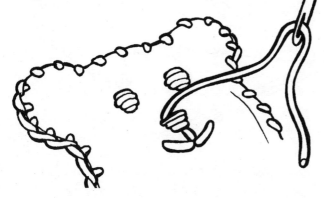

6 Make more shapes and stitch them together in a row or one below the other.

More ideas

● Make just one shape and stitch a loop onto it so it can be hung up on a wall or a doorknob.

● Add sequins, beads, buttons, lace or ribbons to your felt shapes.

● Draw letters on thin cardboard and cut them out. Use them to create a stuffed felt name or word.

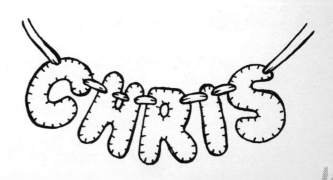

Beeswax candle

Candles made from beeswax are smokeless, dripless and they smell like honey. Best of all, they're easy to make.

1 Place the beeswax on a sheet of waxed paper. Lay the ruler on the beeswax diagonally. Use scissors to mark a light line and cut along this straight edge. Set one triangle aside to make another candle later.

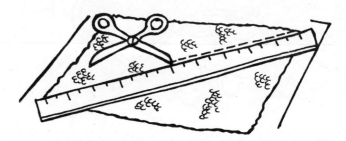

2 Cut a piece of candlewick about 5 cm (2 in.) longer than the shortest side of your triangle. Place the wick along the short edge of the triangle so that some of it hangs over at each end.

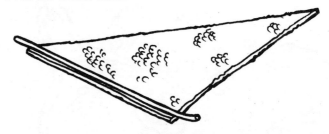

3 Roll and press the edge of the wax into the wick. It helps if your hands are warm. If the wax cracks a little, press it firmly over the wick and it will stick together.

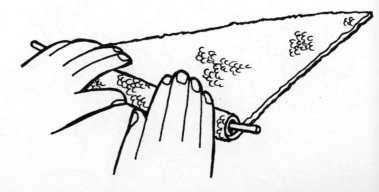

Things you need

- a sheet of beeswax (available at craft and hobby stores)
- waxed paper
- a long ruler or a straight edge
- scissors
- candlewick

4 Tightly roll the wax, keeping the straight edge even.

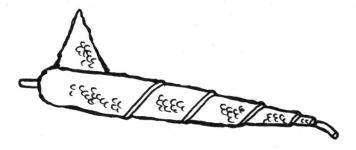

5 As you finish the candle, roll it firmly across the waxed paper to make the end stick in place. If the bottom is uneven, gently push it down to make it flat.

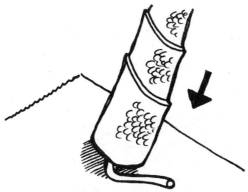

6 Cut off the wick at the bottom and trim it to 1 cm (½ in.) on top. If you are not going to burn the candle now, store it in a sheet of waxed paper.

7 Place the candle in a holder that can fit different-sized candles. Have an adult light the candle, and blow it out before you leave the room.

More ideas

● To make shorter candles, first cut the sheet of beeswax in half lengthwise and then cut it diagonally. Or cut straight strips and simply roll them up with a piece of wick inside. These types of candles may not fit into a regular holder, so set them on a non-flammable surface to burn them.

● Try rolling two colors of wax together. Or roll your candle in glitter sprinkled on a sheet of waxed paper.

● Cut out little wax holly leaves, hearts, stars or other shapes and press them onto your candle to decorate it.

Striped molded candle

The layers of wax used to create the stripes in this candle are colored with crayons.

Things you need

- candlewick
- a paperboard container from frozen juice concentrate
- a pencil and scissors
- candle wax, in bars or shredded (available at craft and hobby stores)
- paperless crayons in different colors
- stearic acid (available at craft and hobby stores)
- tin cans
- a small pot
- masking tape
- oven mitts

1 Cut a piece of wick about 5 cm (2 in.) longer than your juice can is tall. Tape one end of the wick to the inside bottom of the juice can. You may need to use the end of a pencil to pat it down firmly if your hand doesn't fit inside.

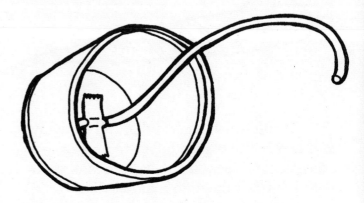

2 Place the pencil across the top of the juice can and tape the top of the wick to it so that the wick is straight.

3 Place about one bar or 250 mL (1 c.) of shredded wax, a crayon and 5 to 10 mL (1 to 2 tsp.) of stearic acid in a tin can. You'll need a different can for each color of wax you make. Any leftover wax can be reheated and used another time.

4 Slightly bend the can to form a spout. Place the can in the pot. Add enough water to the pot to make it come about one-third of the way up the can. Don't put too much water in the pot, or the can might float and tip.

5 Ask an adult to place the pot on the stove and heat it on medium-low. It will melt slowly. Never melt wax on high heat or directly in a pot — it can catch on fire.

6 When the wax has melted, wear oven mitts to remove the pot from the stove. Ask an adult to help you pour the wax carefully into the juice can. (If your wick comes loose, pull it out of the can and dip it into hot wax. Let it cool for a minute and then straighten it with your fingers. It will be hard enough for you to poke into the wax in the juice can.) Allow the layer of wax to cool and harden for at least an hour.

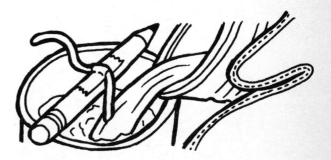

7 Melt more wax with a different-colored crayon. Wait until each layer is hardened before you add another one.

8 When the candle is finished, hard and cool, trim the wick to about 1.5 cm (5/8 in.). Cut and tear away the juice-can mold to see how the candle looks.

Clay-pot candle

This gift is a candle and holder all in one! You can paint the outside of your clay pot ahead of time (see page 108), but you don't need to paint the inside — just the rim.

Things you need

- masking tape
- a small clay pot 5 to 9 cm (2 to 3½ in.) in diameter
- candlewick
- a pencil and scissors
- candle wax, in bars or shredded (available at craft and hobby stores)
- a medium-sized tin can (796 mL [28 oz.] works well)
- a small pot
- oven mitts

1 Put two layers of masking tape across the hole on the inside of your clay pot. Cut a piece of wick about 5 cm (2 in.) longer than your pot is tall. Firmly tape the wick to the center bottom of the pot.

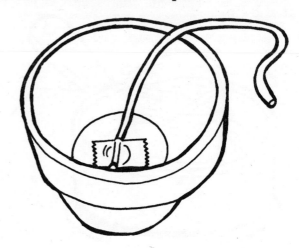

2 Place the pencil across the top of the clay pot and tape the other end of the wick to it so that the wick is straight, but not taut.

3 Place one or two bars of wax in the can (you can break them by using the point of a dull knife), or use 250 to 500 mL (1 to 2 c.) of shredded wax.

4 Slightly bend the can to form a spout. Place the can in the pot. Add enough water to the pot to make it come about one-third of the way up the can. Don't put too much water in the pot, or the can might float and tip.

5 Ask an adult to place the pot on the stove and heat it on medium-low. It will melt slowly. Never melt wax on high heat or directly in a pot — it can catch on fire.

6 When the wax has melted, wear oven mitts to remove the pot from the stove. Ask an adult to help you pour the wax carefully into the clay pot to about 1 cm (1/2 in.) from the top. Allow it to cool and harden. If the wax shrinks as it hardens, you may want to fill in the hollow with a little more melted wax.

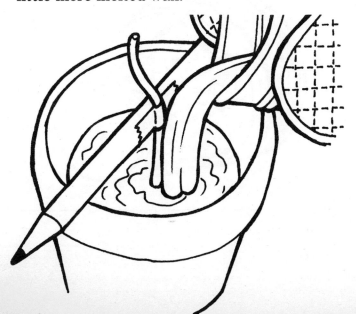

7 When the candle is hard and cool, remove the wick from the pencil and trim it to about 1.5 cm (5/8 in.).

More ideas

● Add color to your candle by placing a paperless crayon in with the wax before you melt it. Choose a color that matches the paint on your pot.

● For a festive clay-pot candle, paint the pot gold on the outside and around the top of the inside. Sprinkle a bit of gold glitter on top of the wax as it hardens.

● Instead of painting the pot, tie on a bow or glue on fabric, rhinestones or other trimmings. Make sure decorations will not be in the way of the flame.

Painted clay pot

You can jazz up old or new clay pots with paint. They are inexpensive at craft and gardening supply stores.

Things you need

- a clay pot
- newspaper or sheet of plastic
- acrylic paints
- a paintbrush
- acrylic varnish

1 Wipe your clay pot with a dry cloth to remove any dust. If you are using an old clay pot and it needs washing, leave it in a warm place to dry overnight.

2 Cover your work surface with newspaper or plastic. Decide on a pattern or a picture to paint on your pot. You may want to draw on scrap paper first to get some ideas.

3 You can paint the whole pot in one color first, let it dry and then begin painting a pattern. Or you can paint directly on the clay surface.

4 When you are finished painting your pot, allow it to dry completely.

5 Clay pots absorb moisture. So, if you're going to plant directly into the pot, apply a couple of coats of acrylic varnish on the inside and outside surfaces first. This will help prevent soil moisture from seeping through the pot and leaving watermarks on your table or causing the paint on your design to bubble. Set the pot on a plastic lid in case any moisture gets through the bottom. Or you can simply use the clay pot as a cover pot and not worry about applying varnish.

More ideas

Use your pot to hold odds and ends, keys, wrapped candies or just for show. Or put a gift in it and tie a ribbon on the pot as your gift "box."

Try sponging a clay pot. Paint the whole pot in one color first. Let it dry and then use a small sponge to dab a second color on top.

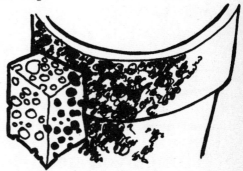

Stencil a pot. See page 182 for how to do stenciling.

109

No-sew lunch bag

This sturdy lunch bag is a great gift for anyone who packs a lunch. If you use plain fabric, you can decorate it with fabric paint before or after making the bag. If you're a sewer, it can be sewn by hand or by machine.

Things you need

- a piece of sturdy fabric such as denim, or strong, lightweight fabric such as nylon, 45 cm x 60 cm (18 in. x 24 in.)

- permanent, washable fabric glue (available at fabric and craft stores)
- a strip of hook-and-loop closure, such as Velcro, about 10 cm (4 in.) long

1 With the fabric good side up, run a line of glue at the edge of each end. Let the glue sit for a couple of minutes. Fold the fabric over so that the glued edges are together. Let this seam dry a little.

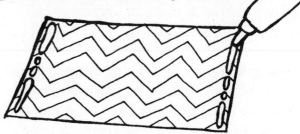

2 Adjust the fabric so that the seam is down the center. Run a line of glue along the seam and on one side of it. Let it sit for a few minutes and then fold the seam over so it is flat. (If you are concerned about the glue soaking through to the inside, put a sheet of waxed paper between the two layers.) Let it dry.

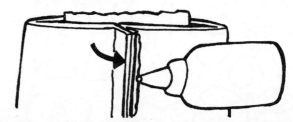

3 On one open end, spread glue about 2.5 cm (1 in.) wide all around the wrong side of the fabric. Fold the raw edge over to make a finished hem. This is the opening of your lunch bag.

4 Again, make sure the seam is down the center. On the other open end, apply glue to the good side (inside) around the opening. Be generous with the glue — it will dry clear.

5 Press the edges together to close the bottom of the lunch bag. Let it dry for about an hour.

6 Place the bag so that the open end is closest to you. Shift it so that the seam is at the right side. Adjust and smooth the top part of the bag until it is in a diamond shape. Apply glue to the corner of the diamond that points towards you.

7 Flip the corner up so it is glued in place. Apply glue to the opposite corner of the diamond and fold it down. Allow these corners to dry for about an hour.

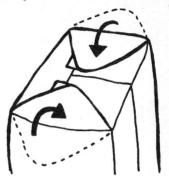

8 Turn the bag right side out. You will see that the bag has a square bottom. Put some glue into each open end. Allow it to dry.

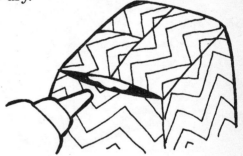

9 Glue the loopy (soft) half of the fastener near the top of one side and the hook half about one-third of the way down on the other side. Make sure the glue is over the edges a little. Allow the closures to dry overnight.

Decorated garden basket

Take an ordinary fruit basket and turn it into a special basket that you can give as a gift or use to hold a gift.

Things you need

- a fruit basket (or any plain basket)
- a measuring tape
- printed cotton or cotton-polyester fabric
- scissors or pinking shears
- white craft glue
- about 20 paper clips
- 1.5 m (5 ft.) of wide ribbon to match the fabric

1 The amount of fabric you'll need depends on the size of your basket. Measure the outside of your basket, going up the end, across the bottom and down the other end. Add 5 cm (2 in.) to this measurement. That's how long your fabric should be.

2 For the width, measure the outside of the basket from the base of one handle, down the side, across the bottom and up to the other handle. Add 5 cm (2 in.) to this measurement.

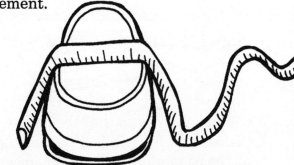

3 Cut two pieces of fabric the size you've measured, and round off the corners. Use pinking shears if you have them, or use scissors and run a thin line of glue around the edges to prevent fraying.

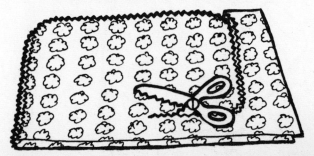

4 Place one piece of fabric good side down and set the basket in the center of it. Run a line of glue around the inside top edge of the basket.

5 Fold the fabric up over the top edge so it is in the glue. Paper clip it in place. Make small pleats at the corners and fold the fabric under at the handles. Let the glue dry.

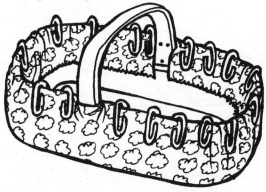

6 Remove the paper clips. Take the other piece of fabric and place it, good side up, inside the basket.

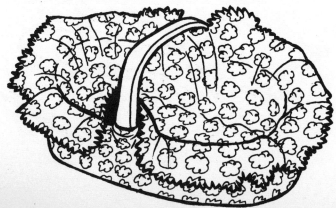

7 You'll notice that some fabric is bunched up around each side at the handle. Cut your ribbon in half and tie it into a bow around the fabric at the base of the handle on each side. This will hold the liner in place as well as add a lovely finishing touch.

8 Spot glue the liner in place all around the basket. Use the paper clips to hold the liner down until the glue is dry.

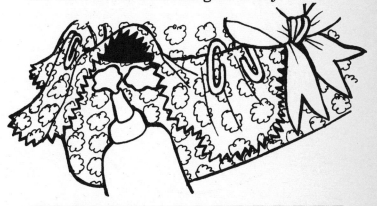

More ideas

⊙ Use two different fabrics to decorate the basket — one to cover the outside and the other to use as a liner.

⊙ Wind ribbon or lace around the handle. Or sew a lace ruffle around the liner before you place it in the basket.

Felt gift bag

This easy-to-sew bag is fun to make and looks terrific. It's reusable, so it can be passed around with different gifts for years.

Things you need

- 2 felt squares
- pins
- a large darning needle
- yarn
- scissors
- ribbon

1 Pin the two felt squares together on three sides, leaving the top open.

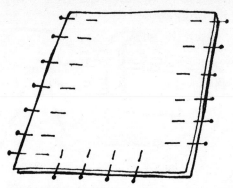

2 Thread the yarn into the needle and knot the yarn. Starting from the inside of the top corner, pull the needle through one layer of felt to the front so the knot won't show.

3 Bring the needle to the back and poke through both layers of felt to the front of the bag. Use the running stitch (see page 202) to sew around the three sides. Remove the pins as you sew.

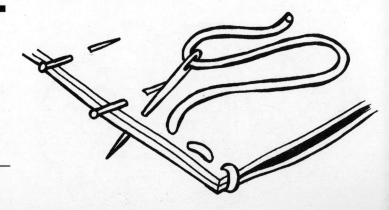

4 When you reach the end, make a few extra stitches on top of the last one and poke the needle through one layer to the inside of the bag. Knot the yarn and cut it.

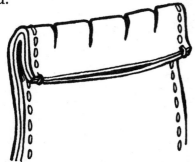

5 Fold down the top of the bag about 5 cm (2 in.). Make four evenly spaced cuts through both layers along this folded edge. Unfold.

6 Starting at the center of the bag, weave the ribbon through the slits. Be sure to leave enough ribbon on each end to tie the bag closed.

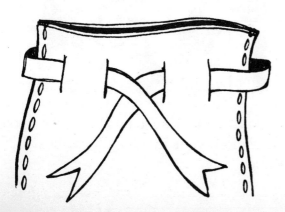

More ideas

⊙ Use two different colors of felt for your bag.

⊙ Make a bag out of regular fabric. Use pinking shears to cut your squares.

⊙ Trick someone by wrapping a small gift in a small bag, within a slightly larger bag, in a larger bag and so on. It will take a while to open the gift!

Gift boxes

Here's an inexpensive, environmentally friendly way to box a gift. You don't need to add wrapping paper, because the box will be fancy enough.

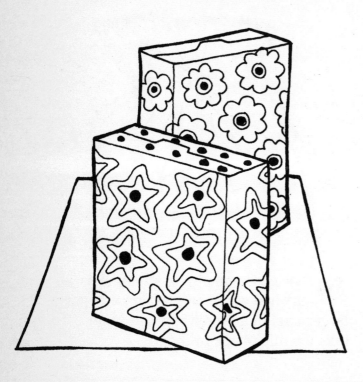

Things you need

- an empty cardboard box such as a cereal or cracker box
- acrylic craft paint
- printing supplies (see page 76–77)
- white craft glue

1 Carefully open both ends of the box. Run your fingers down the glued side seam to undo it.

2 Lay the box flat, inside up. Print or paint the box.

3 Glue the side seam together. You will need to hold it for a couple of minutes. Glue the bottom of the box together and hold it for a while.

4 Use the tab closure on the top to open and close your inside-out gift box. It's reusable.

Gift wrap

If you're going to use wrapping paper, why not make your own?

Things you need

- paper bags
- scissors
- acrylic craft paint
- printing supplies (see page 76–77)

1 If the bag is plain, simply lay it flat and print one side at a time.

2 If the bag is already printed on the outside, cut down one side of the bag and cut out the bottom. Lay it flat and print the plain side.

3 Use the paper to wrap your gift, or put the gift inside the printed bag.

More ideas

For small gifts, a decorated paper lunch bag is just right. Decorate it with printing, drawings, magazine pictures or cut-up used greeting cards. When you are finished, fold down the top. Use a hole punch to make two holes in the folded-down area. Use ribbon or yarn to tie it closed.

Greeting card mini box

There are so many beautiful, scenic, funny and interesting greeting cards around. Here's a simple way to recycle one into a box perfect for a small gift. And you don't need to wrap it because it's already decorated!

Things you need

- a medium-sized rectangular new or used greeting card
- a pencil and a ruler
- scissors
- white craft glue
- 8 paper clips

1 Cut the card in half along its fold line.

2 On the back of the front half of the card, draw a line 2.5 cm (1 in.) in from both sides. Draw a line 4 cm (1½ in.) in from both ends.

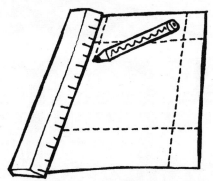

3 Using the ruler as a guide, fold down the two sides along the lines. Open them out and fold down the ends. Open them.

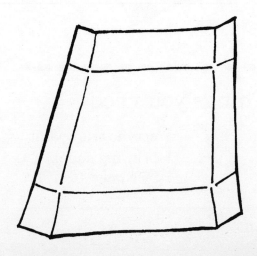

4 Now each corner has a small rectangle. Cut along the longer line of each corner rectangle, just to the folded corner.

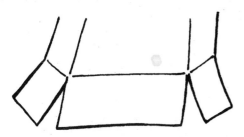

5 Bend the four corner rectangles upright. Bend the sides up so that your box now has four walls.

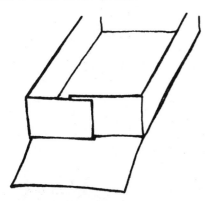

6 To hold the walls in place, bend forward the remaining two pieces. Fold them down over the newly created end walls and glue them in place. Use paper clips to hold the fold until the glue dries.

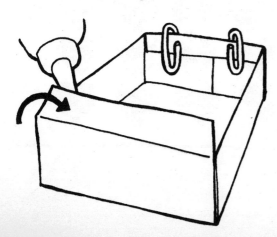

7 Cut a small half-circle thumb notch from each long side of the box lid.

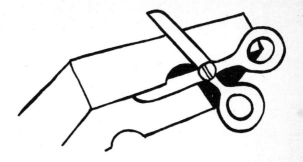

8 To make the bottom of the box, use the other half of the card and very slightly increase the measurements given in step 2 (only by a hair!). Follow steps 2 to 6 and you've finished your mini box.

More ideas

🔘 If there's lots of writing in the card, you could glue in a small rectangle of felt on the bottom or the lid (or both) of the box after you've put it together.

🔘 Make a tiny box by using only the front of the card — cut it in half and use the halves for the top and bottom. Use smaller measurements, too.

Special days

Birthdays, weddings, graduations, anniversaries, new seasons — there are so many special days and holidays to celebrate. You can make them extra-special with the ideas in this section. Keep track of special days by marking them on a homemade calendar. Use handmade paper to print party invitations and original greeting cards. Decorate for the festivities with tissue flowers, clay ornaments, decorated wreaths and baskets. Make a piñata for a fun party game. You can even make a mini photo album to hold photographs of special days and holidays so you can enjoy the memories for years.

Special-days calendar

Since this calendar does not include the days of the week, you can use it for years as a daily reminder of whose birthday, anniversary or special day is coming up.

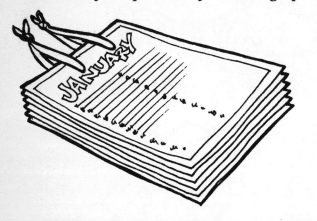

Things you need

- 12 pieces of lined paper, each about 14 cm x 18 cm (5 1/2 in. x 7 in.)
- a pencil, markers or colored pencils
- 6 pieces of heavy paper, bristol board or handmade paper, each about 15 cm x 23 cm (6 in. x 9 in.) (see page 126)
- white craft glue
- a hole punch
- thin ribbon
- scissors
- paper-hole reinforcers (optional)

1 Write a month at the top of each sheet of lined paper. Play with the design of the letters so they suit the time of year.

2 Write half the days of the month down the left-hand side of the sheets. Down the center write the other half of the days. Write twenty-nine days for February, thirty for April, June, September and November, and thirty-one for all the rest.

3 Glue a month sheet to the front and back of each heavy paper sheet.

4 Punch two evenly spaced holes at the top of one heavy sheet. Use it as a guide to punch holes in the other five sheets. It may be necessary to apply hole reinforcers to both sides of your heavy paper, especially if you're using handmade paper.

5 Cut two pieces of ribbon, each 35 cm (14 in.) long. Thread one through each set of holes. Use an overhand knot to tie the ends of each ribbon together.

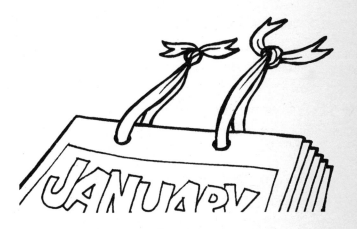

6 Go through your calendar and write the names of family members and friends beside the correct date. Write down their birth year, too, so you'll be reminded of the person's age. You can add names and years any time.

7 To hang up your calendar, hold the ribbon loops together and hang them on the same nail.

Paper maker

To make paper you need a "mold" and a "deckle" that work together to sieve and shape fibers into paper. Here's how to make your own paper maker so you can make paper for greeting cards, gift tags and other special-day projects.

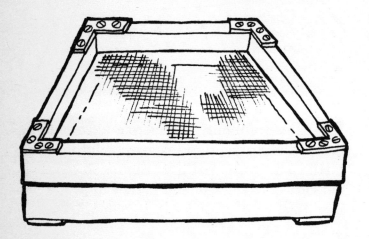

Things you need

- lengths of wood about 2.5 cm (1 in.) wide x 2.5 cm (1 in.) thick
- a ruler and a pencil
- a handsaw
- fine sandpaper

- nails and hammer or 8 flat corner braces, screws and a screwdriver
- fiberglass screen
- scissors
- a stapler

Note: Instead of fastening together pieces of wood, you can use two same-sized wooden picture frames with inside measurements of at least 13 cm x 18 cm (5 in. x 7 in.), but not larger than 20 cm x 25 cm (8 in. x 10 in.). Remove the glass and backing from both and go to step 5.

1 Have an adult help you saw four pieces of wood, each 20 cm (8 in.) long. Cut four more 23 cm (9 in.) long. (Many lumber stores will cut wood for you if you don't have a saw.) Sand the cut ends to make them level and smooth.

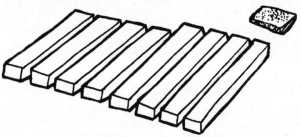

2 Place two short and two long pieces of wood together as shown to form a rectangular frame.

3 Hammer or screw together the frame. Make sure the corners form right angles.

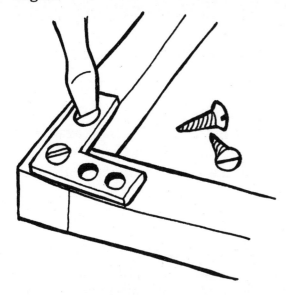

4 Make another frame the same way, using the other four pieces of wood.

5 Cut a piece of screen a little bigger than the frames.

6 Open your stapler and hold it firmly against the wood as you staple along one short side. Pull the screen taut and staple it along the long sides and finally along the other short side.

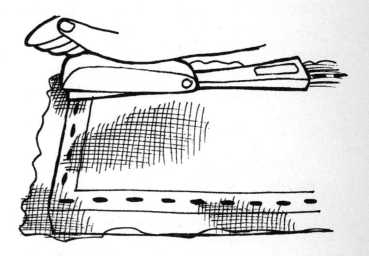

7 Trim the screen so it is even with the frame. This is your mold and the empty frame is your deckle. Turn the page to find out how to make paper with them.

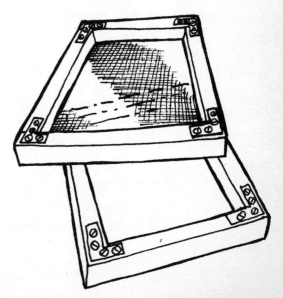

Making paper

You can recycle newspaper, junk-mail flyers, used computer paper, construction paper scraps and even brown paper bags into beautiful handmade paper. Avoid using glossy magazine and catalog paper.

Things you need

- a large bowl or a small plastic pail
- scrap paper
- a blender
- a large dishpan
- a spoon
- a mold and deckle (see page 124)

- smooth absorbent cloths such as old dish towels, strips of old bed sheets or reusable all-purpose kitchen cloths
- a sponge
- a rolling pin
- an iron (optional)

1 Tear paper into small squares and place them in the bowl. You could start with two sheets of newspaper, six sheets of computer paper (try combining white paper with another color), four sheets of construction paper scraps or two medium-sized paper bags.

2 Sift through the paper pieces to make sure the squares aren't stuck together. Cover the paper with hot tap water. The paper will float, so stir it to make it all wet. Let the paper soak for a few hours or overnight.

3 To make pulp, drop a handful of wet paper pieces into the blender. Fill the blender about half full of water and ask an adult to help you blend until it looks like thick soup. Pour it into the dishpan and make more pulp.

4 When all the pulp is in the dishpan, add enough water so that the dishpan is three-quarters full and stir. This mixture is called "slurry."

5 Hold the mold screen side up with the deckle on top. Dip it vertically into the slurry and level it under the water.

7 Hold the paper maker on a slight angle to allow it to drip. When it stops dripping, remove the deckle.

6 Lift the paper maker slowly. When it is still partially under water, check to see if the screen is evenly covered with pulp. If it isn't, gently shake the paper maker back and forth. When the screen is evenly covered, lift the paper maker out of the water and hold it above the dishpan.

8 Turn the mold upside down onto a few layers of flat cloth. Gently dab (don't rub) the back of the screen with the sponge to remove some of the water. Slowly lift the mold, leaving the sheet of paper on the cloth. If the paper sticks to the screen, hold the mold above the cloth and give it a quick, downward shake.

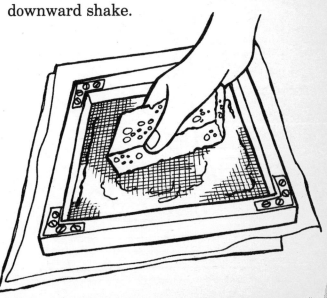

Continued on next page

9 Carefully place another cloth on top of the sheet of paper. Roll over it quickly and lightly with the rolling pin to remove more water and give it a smooth finish. Remove the cloth.

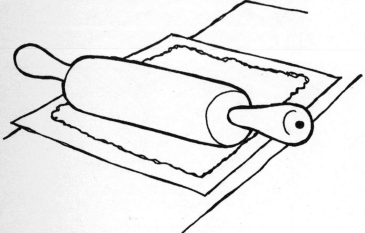

11 There are a few different ways to dry your paper. You can leave it to dry on the cloths for two or three days. Or you can hang the cloth and paper to dry on an indoor line, or outdoors on a calm, warm day. Or ask an adult to iron it between two cloths.

10 Stir the slurry and make more sheets of paper. When you are finished, place the paper maker in the kitchen sink. Slowly pour the slurry through the screen to catch all the leftover pulp (don't let any go down the drain). You should end up with one last sheet of paper.

12 When the paper (and cloths) are dry, gently lift one corner and peel the paper from the cloth. If any of the sheets of paper are buckled when they are dry, you can place them under a couple of heavy books overnight or iron them between two cloths.

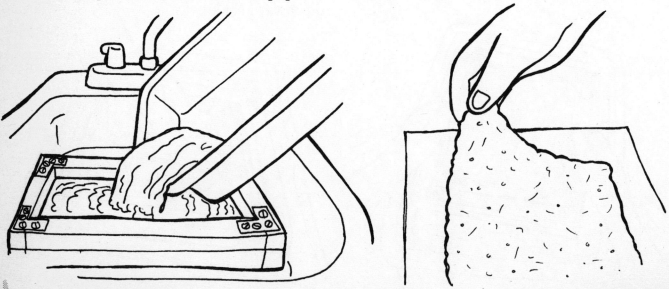

More ideas

Add dried flower petals, glitter, pieces of thread or yarn, small feathers, or bits of tissue or color comics to the slurry.

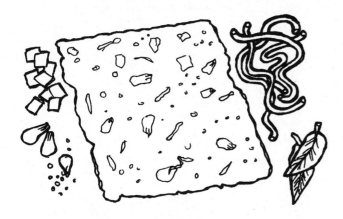

Emboss your paper. Just before rolling the paper (step 9), place a leaf, length of lace, plastic stencil, buttons, key, yarn or some other flat, textured item on the paper. Cover the paper with a cloth and firmly roll over it with the rolling pin.

For colored paper, add a few drops of food coloring to the wet paper pieces in the blender.

To make shapes, set the mold (without the deckle) in the sink. Hold a cookie cutter on the screen. Use a cup to scoop slurry from the dishpan into the cookie cutter. When it stops dripping, remove the cookie cutter and continue.

You can even make paper from dryer lint. You don't need to use a blender. Start at step 4, using lint instead of pulp. This cloth-like paper is not suitable for writing on, but can be used as a background in a picture frame or as a card with another piece of paper glued inside.

Pressed-flower card

Make a few of these cards to have ready for unexpected special days. See page 136 for how to make envelopes.

Things you need

- construction paper, blank index card or handmade paper (see page 126)
- clear, self-adhesive plastic
- a pencil and scissors
- pressed flowers (see page 86)
- rubber cement or white craft glue

1 Cut and fold your paper to the size you want your card to be.

2 Trace the folded card on the backing of the plastic and cut out the plastic.

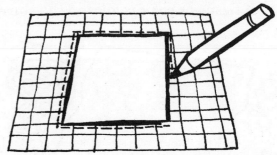

3 Arrange pressed flowers on the front of the card using tiny dabs of glue to hold them in place.

4 Peel away the paper backing and cover the front of the card with the plastic. Trim any extra plastic around the edges.

5 Write your initials or a clever company name on the back of the card so everyone will know it is hand made.

Woven card

Weave your creativity all through this card. It will be suitable for almost any occasion.

1 Cut and fold the paper to the size you want your card to be.

2 Open the card and place it on the cardboard. Use scissors or the X-acto knife to slice rows of slits into the front of the card. The rows can go in any direction, but should not reach the edges.

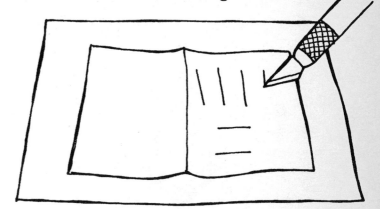

3 Cut or tear strips of paper that will fit through the slits on the card.

4 Weave the strips in and out of the slits. Glue down the ends of the strips to the front and inside of the card. Or try weaving ribbon or strips of wrapping paper into the card.

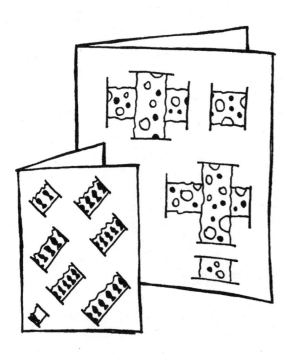

Things you need

- paper (handmade paper works well, see page 126)
- cardboard
- scissors or an X-acto knife
- white craft glue
- ribbon or wrapping paper (optional)

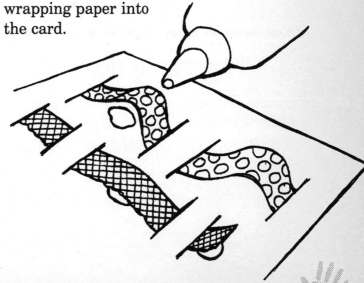

Heart-strings card

This card is a decoration as well as a greeting.

Things you need

- 2 sheets of paper in different colors
- a pencil
- scissors
- embroidery floss
- white craft glue
- markers, glitter or other decorating supplies

1 Hold both pieces of paper together and fold them in half. Draw a large half-heart along the fold.

2 Cut out your hearts, but before opening them, draw another half-heart inside the large one.

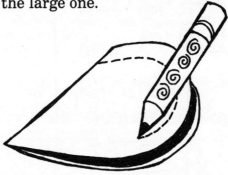

3 Cut out these hearts, but before opening them, draw on a small half-heart. Cut them out. You should have two large, two medium and two small hearts.

4 Cut one piece of embroidery floss 50 cm (20 in.) long and cut two more pieces, each 20 cm (8 in.) long. Fold the long piece in half.

5 Glue the cut ends of the folded floss on a small heart so that the looped end is above the heart. Glue a short piece of floss at the pointed end of the heart.

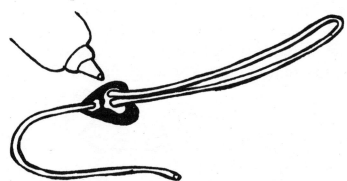

6 Glue the other small heart on top.

7 Attach the medium and large hearts in a similar way so you end up with a string of three hearts.

8 Decorate to your heart's desire. Write your messages on either side of any or all of the hearts.

Party prints

By designing and printing your own invitations, you can be sure they're original. Use these ideas for making note and greeting cards, too. See page 136 for how to make envelopes.

Things you need

- blank 13 cm x 20 cm (5 in. x 8 in.) index cards or blank paper
- a new art gum or white vinyl eraser
- an X-acto knife
- a pencil
- ink stamp pads in different colors
- scrap paper

1 Fold your paper to make a card and put it aside.

2 Cut your eraser into a square shape. Draw a couple of straight thick lines in any direction on your eraser.

3 Carefully cut them out by slanting the X-acto knife so that the edges do not get undercut. When a thick line is cut out, it should look like a V from the side.

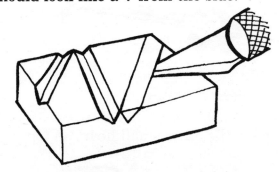

4 Press the eraser down on the stamp pad a few times, then stamp it on scrap paper. If you're not pleased with your design, do some more cutting.

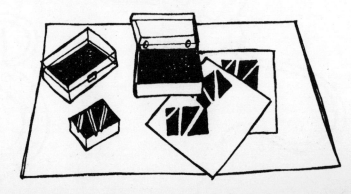

5 Experiment with your design. Stamp it once, turn it a quarter turn and stamp it again; turn and stamp two more times. Leave spaces between the rows, make a border or cover an area completely.

6 When you want to change ink colors, get all the ink off the eraser by stamping it over and over again on scrap paper.

7 When you write out your invitations, be sure to include the party date, time, location, phone number, theme and anything you wish your guests to bring.

More ideas

● Use your eraser stamp to make gift tags and wrapping paper, too.

● Try cutting other eraser designs such as balloons, stars, flowers or hearts.

Handmade envelopes

If you don't have envelopes for cards you've made, here's how to make them.

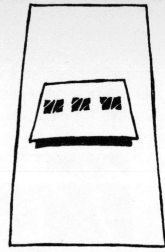

1 Lay the paper vertically and place your card sideways in the center.

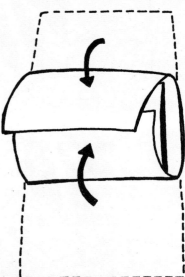

2 Fold the bottom edge up over the card, and the top edge down over the card. Leave a bit of space between the fold and the top edge of the card.

3 Fold the sides in, leaving a bit of space between the card and each fold so it will be easy to slip the card in and out of the envelope.

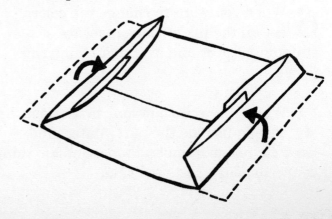

Things you need

- a piece of paper 22 cm x 27 cm (8½ in. x 11 in.)
- a handmade invitation or greeting card
- scissors
- white craft glue or a glue stick

4 Unfold the paper and put aside the card. Cut out the rectangles formed by the folds in each corner.

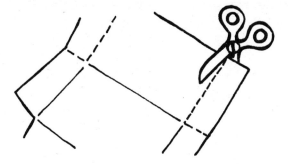

5 Refold the envelope, but this time fold the side pieces in first, then fold the bottom piece up and finally fold the top flap down. Trim off any paper that hangs over an edge or gets in the way of the folding.

6 Lightly glue the bottom piece in place at the sides. Don't use too much glue or your envelope will be stuck shut.

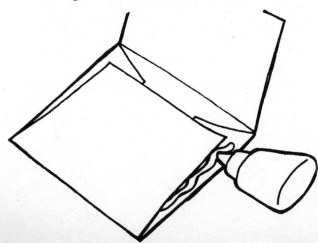

7 If the top flap is large enough, you can round off, scallop or zigzag the edge.

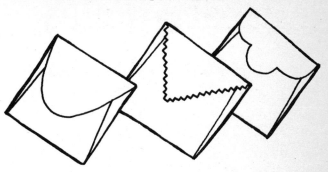

8 To use the envelope, slip the card inside and lightly glue down the flap. If you aren't sending it in the mail, you could seal it with a sticker instead.

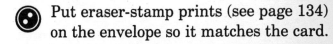

More ideas

🔘 Put eraser-stamp prints (see page 134) on the envelope so it matches the card.

Creative clay

This clay is easy to make and fun to work with. After you've made a batch, turn the page for some great ideas of what to make with it.

Things you need

- a small pot
- cornstarch
- baking soda
- a spoon
- a bowl
- a damp kitchen cloth
- a sealed bowl or a plastic bag

1 In the pot, mix together 125 mL (½ c.) of cornstarch and 250 mL (1 c.) of baking soda. Add 175 mL (¾ c.) of water. Stir the mixture until it is smooth and no longer feels stuck to the bottom of the pot.

2 Ask an adult to help you cook the mixture over medium-low heat, stirring constantly. After a few minutes, the mixture will start to thicken. When it looks like smooth, thick mashed potatoes, turn off the stove and remove the pot.

3 Spoon the ball of clay into a bowl. Add the leftover bits from the pot to the ball. Cover the bowl with the damp cloth to cool.

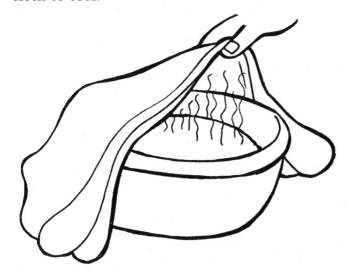

4 When the clay is cool, knead it on a smooth surface dusted with cornstarch. Knead in a little more corn starch if it feels sticky, or leave it out uncovered for an hour or so.

5 Store the creative clay in a sealed bowl or bag. It will keep for a couple of weeks in the fridge. Bring it to room temperature before you use it.

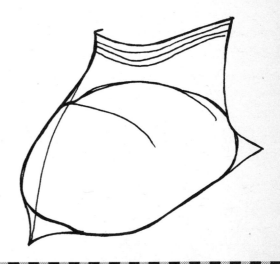

More ideas

⊙ If you want colored clay, add food coloring to the water before you mix it with the starch and soda.

⊙ For marbled clay, add one or two drops of food coloring to a small portion of clay, but don't mix it in too much. Or make two batches of colored clay and lightly mix them together.

⊙ This recipe can be doubled successfully. Work with small amounts at a time and keep the rest covered in a sealed container.

Clay creations

Creative clay can be shaped, rolled, cut, painted and decorated in endless ways. Follow these instructions to make a pendant or special-day ornaments. Then try the other ideas to make a mini frame, buttons and beads.

Things you need

- creative clay (see page 138)
- waxed paper
- foil (optional)
- a rolling pin
- cookie cutters
- a butter knife
- a cookie sheet
- a drinking straw
- acrylic paint and a brush
- fine ribbon or yarn

1 Roll some clay out to a thickness of 0.5 cm (1/4 in.) on a sheet of waxed paper. If the dough sticks to the rolling pin, rub on a bit of cornstarch.

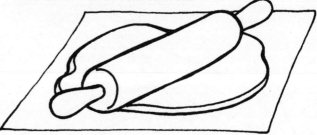

2 Use a knife or cookie cutters to cut out shapes.

3 Transfer them to a cookie sheet lined with waxed paper. (Line the cookie sheet with foil if you want to dry them in the oven.)

4 Use a straw to poke a hole in the center top of each cutout. Leave them in a warm place to dry for a day or two or place them in the oven at 120°C (250°F) for a couple of hours.

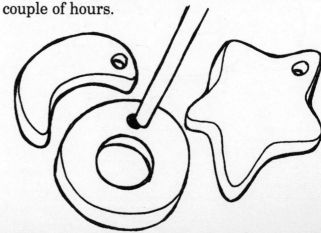

5 Paint your creations and thread ribbon or yarn through the holes.

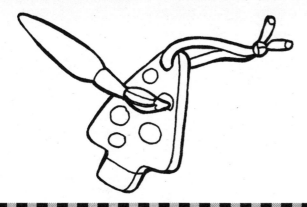

━━━━━━━━━━━━━━━━━━━━━━

More ideas

⊙ Use cutouts for different special days. For example, leaves for fall, flowers for spring, tree ornaments for Christmas or a heart pendant for Valentine's Day.

⊙ Make a mini frame. Cut out a large shape with a small shape in the center. Poke a hole in the top in the middle. Paint and decorate it with sequins, buttons, beads or rhinestones. Tape or glue a photograph to the back.

⊙ Make a few cutouts that can be used to make a mobile or to attach to a wreath.

⊙ Cut mini shapes with toothpick holes and hang them on hoops for earrings.

⊙ Roll small bits of clay in the palm of your hand to make beads. Roll tiny beads between your fingers and thumb. Use a round toothpick to poke in holes.

⊙ Attach a magnet to the back of a clay shape or mini frame and stick it on the fridge.

Tissue-dyed eggs

The secret to these beautiful, colorful eggs is in the tissue paper. Some colors of tissue work better than others — test small pieces on a white sheet of paper.

Things you need

- washed white eggs
- a long darning needle
- 2 small bowls
- assorted scraps of craft tissue paper
- scissors
- drink bottle lids

1 Poke a small hole in each end of an egg. To make it easier to blow out the yolk, poke the needle farther into one end to break the yolk.

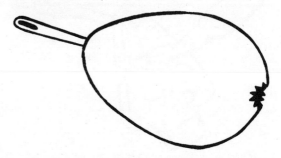

2 Blow the contents of the egg into a small bowl. (Use the eggs for baking or make scrambled eggs.)

3 Rinse out the egg with water and blow out the water.

4 Cut or tear the tissue paper into small pieces.

5 Pour some water into the other bowl. Lightly dip a piece of tissue into the water and quickly stick it onto the egg.

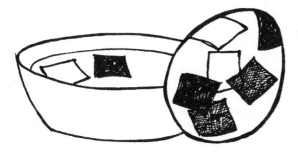

6 Dip and stick pieces of tissue all over the egg. Set it on a bottle lid to dry.

7 When the egg is dry, the pieces of tissue will fall away when you touch them, leaving interesting colors. When your eggs are not on display, store them in an egg carton.

More ideas

These eggs look great in a basket or hanging up. To hang up your eggs, knot a piece of thread around a toothpick. Dab some glue on the knot. Cut off both ends of the toothpick so you have a very short piece. Push this piece into one of the holes in the egg. Pull up on the thread so the toothpick piece is now sideways. Hang up your egg.

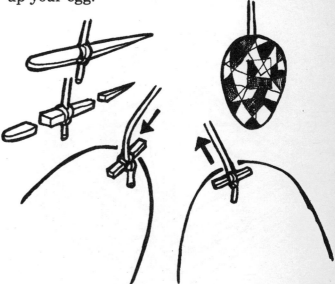

These decorated eggs also look great hanging from, or securely glued onto, a springtime wreath.

Twig basket

This basket can display everything from tissue-dyed eggs (see page 142) to treasures found at the beach. Or leave off the handle and use it as a plant holder. Use only fallen twigs (not taken from a live tree) dry and small enough around that you can break them with your hands.

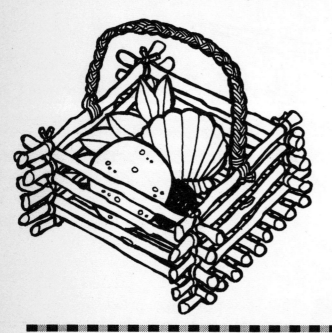

Things you need

- jute, twine or thick yarn
- 30 to 40 dry twig and branch pieces, each about 20 cm (8 in.) long
- a ruler
- scissors
- white craft glue

1 Cut six pieces of twine, each about 1 m (3 ft.) long.

2 Place two twigs horizontally about 15 cm (6 in.) apart. Place two more twigs vertically on top of these twigs.

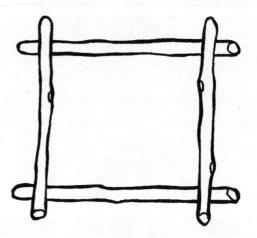

3 Use a piece of twine to fasten each corner together. Knot the twine and leave the ends hanging.

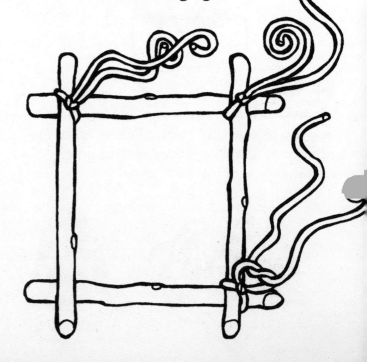

4 Place a row of twigs between the vertical twigs to form a bottom for your basket.

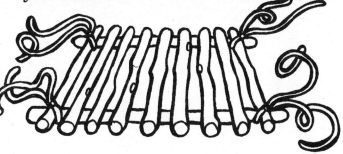

5 Starting at one of the original vertical twigs, use another one of the pieces of twine to tie each twig to the one beside it. Knot the twine to the other original vertical twig and trim the twine. Dab glue on the knot to secure it. Repeat on the other side.

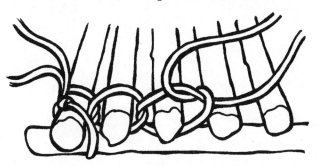

6 To make the sides of the basket, place twigs horizontally above the first twigs. Use the twine at the corners to tie the twigs in place.

7 Place twigs vertically across the new twigs and use the corner twine pieces to tie them in place, too. Keep building the sides of the basket until it is as high as you want it to be.

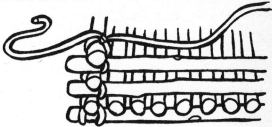

8 Knot the twine at each corner and add a dab of glue to secure each knot. Trim the twine ends.

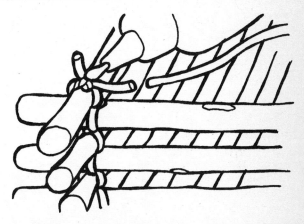

9 Take extra lengths of twine and braid them together to make a handle. Tie the handle across the basket from side to side or corner to corner.

Woven heart basket

This felt variation of a traditional Danish basket can be filled with treats and displayed, or it can be given as a gift for a special day.

Things you need

- 2 squares of different-colored felt
- a ruler
- scissors
- narrow satin ribbon to match the felt

1 Cut a rectangle 6 cm x 20 cm (2 1/4 in. x 8 in.) out of each square of felt.

2 Fold the rectangles in half. Hold each one so that the open edges are at the top. Round off the top corners.

3 Cut two slits up from the folded edge, making them 2 cm (3/4 in.) apart and 7 cm (2 3/4 in.) long.

4 Start weaving one part into the other. Tuck 1 between the layers of C, tuck B between the layers of 1, and 1 between the layers of A. Slide the woven part up a little and now tuck C between 2, 2 between B, and A between 2. Finally, tuck 3 inside C, B inside 3, and 3 inside A. You should see the pattern on the inside as well as on the front and back when you open your basket.

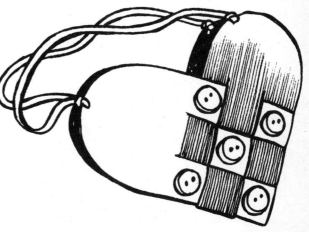

5 Cut a tiny slit at the top of each side of each heart. Tie on ribbon handles.

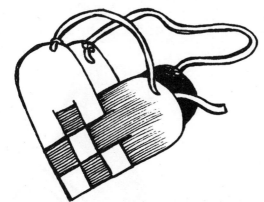

6 Fill your basket with nuts, candies or other treats. Or use it as a tree decoration.

More ideas

Try many felt color combinations. Decorate the heart basket with sewn-on buttons or glued-on rhinestones and beads. Use fabric paint to write on a name or a fancy design.

These baskets can also be made out of shiny paper. The traditional colors are red and white.

Gather a bunch of friends and have a basket-making bee. Make enough baskets for wedding or party favors.

Fabulous fabric wreath

A wreath makes a wonderful, warm welcome to guests arriving for a party. It's also a great way to decorate for special days.

1 Bend a wire hanger into a circle.

2 Cut a strip of fabric 2.5 cm x 50 cm (1 in. x 20 in.). Tape it near the end of the wire and wind it so that it covers the end of the hook and the tape.

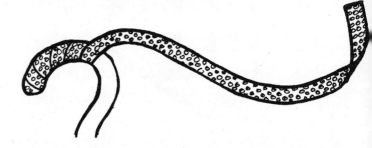

3 Wind the fabric down the straight part of the hook and tape or tie it at the start of the circle.

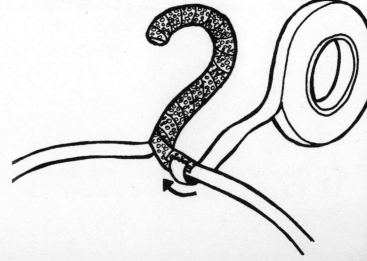

Things you need

- a wire clothes hanger
- scissors or pinking shears
- fabric
- a ruler
- masking tape

4 Tear or cut fabric into strips about 18 cm x 6 cm (7 in. x 2 ¼ in.). You will need about 90 strips.

5 Tie the strips onto the circle. Tie them tightly once — they don't need to be knotted.

6 Slide the fabric strips around the wire until they are packed on tightly. Fluff them and trim off any loose threads. Hang up your new wreath.

7 To store your wreath, cover it with a plastic bag, poke the hanger out through the bottom of the bag and hang it in a closet.

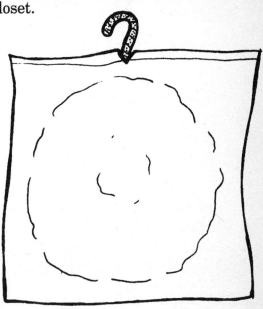

More ideas

Decorate your wreath with ribbon or fabric bows, ornaments or silk leaves and flowers.

149

A wreath for all seasons

Here are instructions for making a basic wreath, followed by ideas for how to decorate it to suit any season.

1 Cut a piece of wire about 15 cm (6 in.) long.

2 Gather together a small bunch of dried or silk flowers. Fasten them into a bundle with the piece of wire.

3 Place the bundle on the wreath to figure out how many flower bundles you will need to cover it. Cut wire and fasten together enough flower bundles to decorate your wreath.

Things you need

- thin wire
- heavy duty scissors or wire-cutters
- silk or dried flowers that you've purchased or dried yourself (see page 88)
- a (grape) vine wreath, any size (available at craft stores)
- ribbon (optional)
- white craft glue (optional)

4 Cut longer pieces of wire, each one long enough to fasten a bundle onto the wreath.

5 Fasten a bundle of flowers onto the wreath. Fasten a second bundle so it covers the stems and wire of the first.

6 Continue to wire and overlap the bundles around the wreath. When you are back where you started, tuck the stems of the last bundle under the flowers of the first bundle.

7 Hold your wreath against a wall or door. Turn it carefully to decide what will be at the top. Fasten a wire loop on the back in the right position.

8 If you like, you can finish your wreath by wiring or gluing on a bow.

Continued on next page

More ideas

For a winter wreath, use lots of greenery with cones, nuts, bright ribbons, artificial birds, small ornaments and cinnamon sticks.

For spring, choose bright silk flowers such as daffodils and tulips with light-colored bows, pussy willows or a pom-pom bunny (see page 168).

● For summer, try dried roses, peonies, straw flowers and daisies.

● For fall, use pressed leaves (see page 86), stalks of wheat, corn husks, small gourds and a variety of dried weeds.

Wedding or shower flowers

Traditionally, these flowers are made out of facial tissues so they look soft and full. For more vibrant colors, use craft tissue paper. If you are hanging them outside or would like to use them for more than one special occasion, make them from colorful plastic bags.

Things you need

- embroidery floss, yarn or strong string
- scissors
- 2-ply facial tissues, tissue paper or plastic bags

1 Cut a piece of embroidery floss about 30 cm (12 in.) long.

2 Cut two facial tissues in half so you have four rectangles. If you are using tissue paper or plastic bags, you will need to cut out six rectangles, each the size of half a facial tissue.

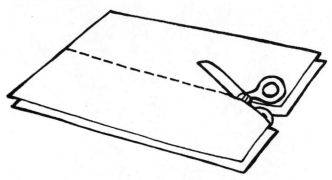

3 Keep the edges straight as you layer the rectangles on top of one another.

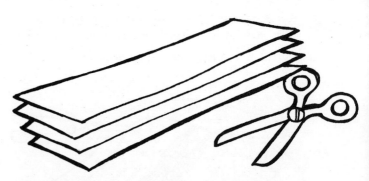

4 Starting at one of the short ends, use small folds to fanfold the layers together.

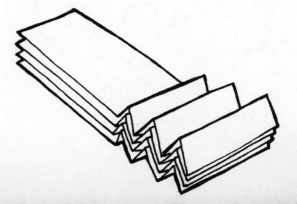

5 Tie the folded layers in the center tightly so you have a bow shape. Double knot the ties.

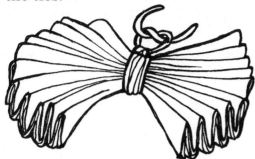

6 Starting at one corner, separate the folded layers, pulling them towards the tied center. If you are using facial tissue, be careful not to tear it as you separate the two plies.

7 When all the layers are separated, hold the tying threads in one hand and pull the flower through your other hand to make it fuller and to create a flat back that is easy to tie or tape to a surface.

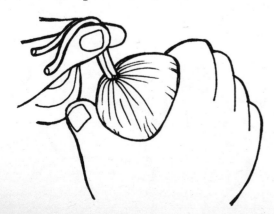

More ideas

⊙ Tie together the fanfolded layers with long pieces of curly ribbon.

⊙ Tie together two flowers, back-to-back, for one large, round flower.

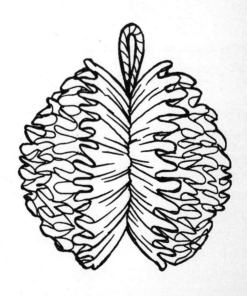

155

Piñata

A piñata adds fun to any special occasion. Save the piñata-breaking game for near the end of the party so everyone can enjoy looking at it for as long as possible.

Things you need

- newspaper
- a ruler and scissors
- a medium-sized round or oval balloon
- 2 mixing bowls, 1 small and 1 medium
- flour and salt
- string or yarn
- tissue paper in many colors
- a pencil with an eraser
- white craft glue

1 Spread newspaper on your work table. Tear other sheets of newspaper into strips about 4 cm x 20 cm (1 ½ in. x 8 in.).

2 Blow up the balloon and knot it. Sit it on the small mixing bowl.

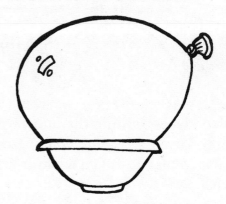

3 To make papier-mâché paste, mix together 175 mL (¾ c.) of flour, 30 mL (2 tbsp.) of salt and 350 mL (1 ½ c.) of water in the other bowl. Use your fingers to get out the lumps.

4 Dip a newspaper strip into the paste and run it between your fingers to get off the extra paste. Smooth the strip onto the balloon.

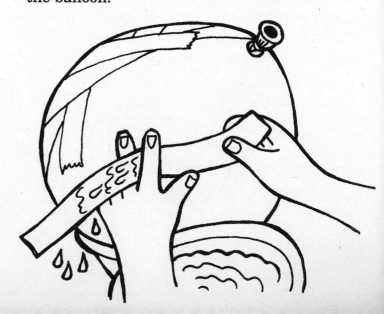

5 Criss-cross pasted strips on the balloon except for an area about 8 cm (3 in.) around the knot. Turn the balloon on the bowl as you work. If the balloon gets too wet, smooth on some dry strips. You should have four or five layers of newspaper on the balloon.

6 Leave it on the bowl and turn it every few hours, or place it on a cooling rack to dry. Depending on how wet your piñata is, it will take from 16 to 48 hours to dry. When you are sure it is dry (check by feeling around the open edge), pop the balloon and take it out.

7 Use scissors to poke three evenly spaced holes 2.5 cm (1 in.) from the top. Cut three pieces of yarn or string, each 1 m (3 ft.) long. Pull one piece halfway through each hole and knot all six ends together.

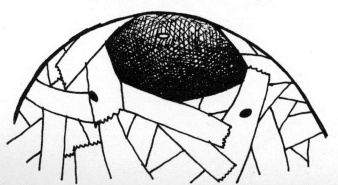

8 Cut sheets of tissue paper into 8 cm x 8 cm (3 in. x 3 in.) squares. Poke the eraser end of your pencil into the center of a square of tissue paper, scrunch the tissue around the pencil and dip it into glue.

9 Press the tissue onto the piñata. Cover the outside of your piñata with these tissue-paper tufts. When you are finished, glue a few long strips of tissue paper to the bottom of the piñata for decoration.

10 Put in wrapped candies or other surprises such as bracelets and scrunchees that you've made yourself from instructions in this book. Be careful not to make your piñata too heavy. Hang it from the ceiling or tie it on a stick and have someone hold it up high.

Piñata party

Everyone stands in a circle around the piñata. One player at a time is blindfolded, turned around three times and given a stick. Each player has three chances to try to whack the piñata. Everyone takes turns until someone breaks the piñata and the goodies spill out. All the players share the treats!

Mini photo album

It's nice to have a photo album full of pictures from one special occasion or time. Make one for each special event, such as a birthday, wedding or summer vacation.

Things you need

- regular or construction paper in one or many colors
- a pencil, a ruler and scissors
- a hole punch

- heavy paper or handmade paper (see page 126)
- narrow ribbon, embroidery floss or yarn
- self-adhesive photo corners or masking tape

1 Place a photograph on a sheet of paper. Mark an area 2.5 cm (1 in.) around the photograph.

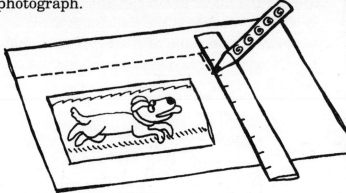

2 Cut out the piece of paper. Use it as a guide to cut out as many more sheets as you need.

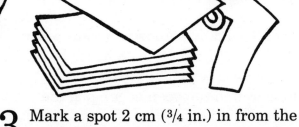

3 Mark a spot 2 cm (³/₄ in.) in from the side and 2 cm (³/₄ in.) down from the top left corner on one of the sheets. Do the same for the bottom left corner.

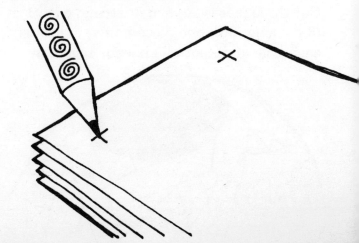

4 Punch a hole at each mark. Use this sheet as a guide for where to punch holes in the other sheets.

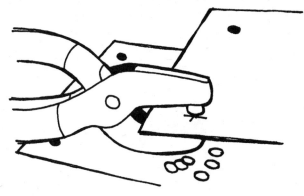

5 From the heavy or handmade paper, cut out front and back covers the same size or slightly larger than the photo sheets. Punch holes in them to match the holes in the sheets.

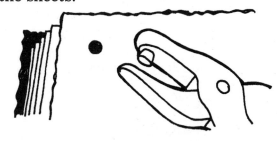

6 Cut two pieces of ribbon or yarn, each about 50 cm (20 in.) long. Put the photo album together so that all the punched holes line up.

7 Starting at the bottom left corner, poke the ribbon down through all the holes, up and around the bottom edge and down through the holes again. Pull on the ribbon ends to make them even and tie them in a double-knot bow at the side.

8 Tie the top left corner the same way.

9 Slip the photo corners onto a photograph. Place it on an album page and press down on each corner to secure it. You can also use masking tape loops on the backs of the photos. Fill your album and label each photo.

Old-time crafts

Here's your chance to make some of the crafts your grandparents did. It's amazing how many old-time crafts have stood the test of time and are still popular today. Some crafts, such as making a hobbyhorse, hand puppet, Jacob's ladder or yarn doll, make terrific toys and decorations. Other crafts, such as embroidery, stenciling and weaving, have always been handy skills to have. Use them to embroider a sampler, stencil a napkin or weave a placemat. Many crafts, such as corking and making pom-pom animals, have likely survived because they are just plain old-fashioned fun.

Jacob's ladder

This old-time toy is as much fun to make now as it was years ago. Ask an adult to help you with the saw, or ask at a lumber store if they will cut the wooden blocks for you.

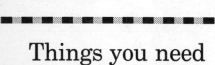

Things you need

- 6 wooden blocks, each about 8 cm (3 in.) long, 5 cm (2 in.) wide and 0.5 cm (¼ in.) thick
- fine sandpaper
- 15 pieces of satin ribbon, each about 1 cm (³⁄₈ in.) wide and 13 cm (5 in.) long
- white craft glue

1 Sand each of the wooden blocks so the corners and edges are smooth and rounded.

2 On each of five of the blocks, glue three pieces of ribbon, as shown. Allow them to dry.

3 Turn the blocks over and line them up so that the single-ribbon ends and the double-ribbon ends are all sitting the same way. Position all the ribbons so they are straight out from each end.

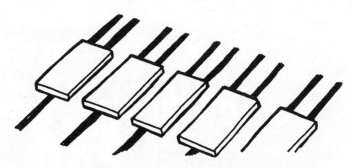

4 On one block, bring all three ribbons across the plain top of the block so a short part of each of the three ribbons is hanging over the opposite edge.

5 Set another block on top of the first so that the two blocks are perfectly lined up. Gently pull up the three short ribbon ends and lightly glue them down on the top surface of this second block.

6 As you did for the first block, bring the three ribbons across the second block to the opposite edge. Place another block on top and glue down the short ribbon ends.

7 Continue in this way, allowing a bit of drying time between blocks. The last block will be the plain one. Simply glue the short ribbon ends in place.

8 To make your Jacob's ladder work, pick up the top block of the pile and hold the blocks in a line with the side edges facing you. Tip down the top block until it almost touches the second one. This will make the blocks look and sound as if they are tumbling down. To make it go again, tip the top block down the other way and they'll tumble down again.

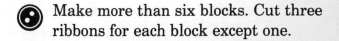

More ideas

🔘 For colorful blocks, paint each one before you glue on the ribbons, or try ribbons of many different colors.

🔘 Make more than six blocks. Cut three ribbons for each block except one.

Hobbyhorse

Families have been enjoying old-fashioned hobbyhorses for generations. Make one using the leftover sock your new-fangled washing machine didn't eat!

1 Tape the rag over the end of the stick. Tightly stuff the foot of the sock. Put the stick in the sock and stuff all around it.

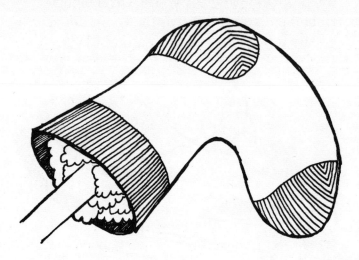

2 Apply glue to the inside top of the sock and the stick. Tightly wind yarn over the glued area and knot it.

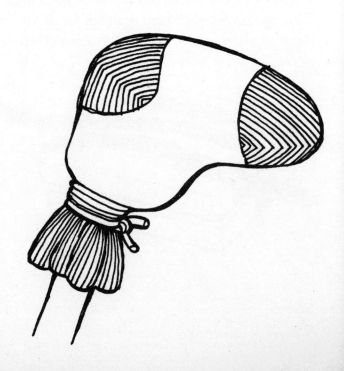

Things you need

- a broomstick or wooden dowel
- a small, clean rag
- strong tape
- an adult-sized sock in good shape
- polyester fiber stuffing
- white craft glue
- yarn
- scraps of felt
- scissors
- 2 buttons
- a needle and thread
- a darning needle
- ribbon

3 Cut two felt circles for eyes and sew a button onto each one. Stitch the eyes onto the horse's head. Make a couple of tiny stitches as you finish so the other stitches don't come loose.

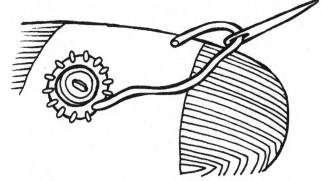

4 Cut out two felt triangles, with rounded sides, for ears. Fold each ear in half and stitch one onto each side of the sock.

5 Cut out two more felt circles for the nostrils. Sew or glue one onto each side of your horse's muzzle.

6 Use yarn and a darning needle to make a mane. Poke the needle in and bring it back out close by. Pull the yarn through and snip it, leaving yarn ends on both sides. Knot the ends together.

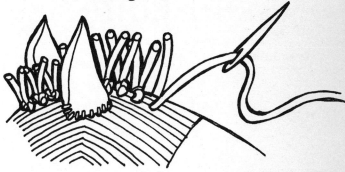

7 Continue cutting and tying until the mane is all the way down the horse's neck.

8 To make reins, tie a length of ribbon around your horse's muzzle. Bring one of the ribbon ends around each side of the horse's head and tie the ribbon together.

Making pom-poms

Once you've tried this simple way of making pom-poms, turn the page to find some great things to make with them.

1 Cut a piece of yarn about as long as your arm. Cut it in half. Set this yarn aside.

2 Hold your index and middle fingers of one hand slightly apart as you very loosely start winding yarn from the ball around them.

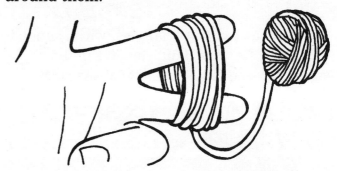

3 Depending on the size of your fingers and the thickness of the yarn, you will need to wind the yarn between 50 and 100 times. Wind it loosely enough so that it doesn't hurt, and keep a space in between your fingers. Cut the yarn from the ball.

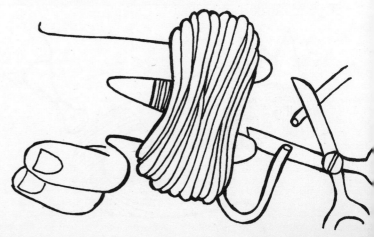

4 Take the pieces of yarn you cut and push them in between your fingers on each side of the wound yarn. Tie them loosely with a double loop, as shown.

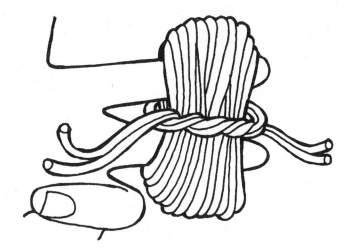

5 Gently slide the yarn off your fingers. Tie the yarn as tightly as you can in the center of the bundle of yarn. Triple knot the tying yarn as shown.

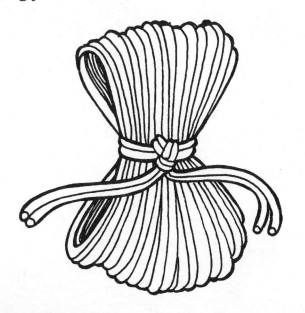

6 Cut open all the loops and trim your pom-pom. Hit it against the edge of a table to fluff it and see if it needs any more trimming. The more you trim your pom-pom, the smaller and thicker it will get. Don't trim off the tying yarn ends — you may need them to tie your pom-pom onto another project.

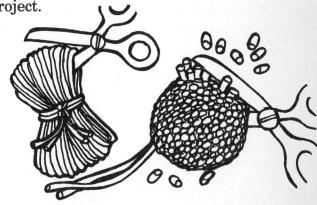

More ideas

- Experiment with many types and thicknesses of yarn.

- To make a striped pom-pom, use two colors of yarn. Wind a large section of each color around your fingers. Use variegated yarn or leftovers of many colors of yarn for a multicolored pom-pom.

- If you want a large pom-pom, wind the yarn around three or four of your fingers.

167

Pom-pom bunny

Traditional pom-pom animals such as this bunny or a chick look great on a wreath, a gift box or in a homemade basket. Make lots!

Things you need

- yarn
- scissors
- white craft glue
- felt scraps
- beads or roly eyes

1 Make one small and one medium-sized pom-pom (see page 166). Use the tying yarn to tightly knot the two pom-poms together, and then trim it off.

2 Cut out long felt ears. Use scissors to poke open an area on the small pom-pom to glue in the ears. Glue on bead, felt or roly eyes.

3 For the nose and whiskers, cut four strands of yarn, each about 5 cm (2 in.) long. Knot them together in the center. Trim them and glue them in place.

4 Make a tiny pom-pom puff for the tail and glue it in place. Trim the bottom of the big pom-pom to keep your bunny from rolling over, or glue on felt feet.

Yarnyard animals

Chick

Make one small and one medium-sized pom-pom. Knot them together with the tying yarn. Make a diamond-shaped beak from felt, fold it in half and glue it in place. Glue on felt, bead or roly eyes and a tail feather. Glue on two bent pipe-cleaner pieces for feet.

Pig

Make one medium and one large-sized pom-pom. Knot them together. Glue on eyes, a two-hole button nose and a yarn smile. Glue on four short pieces of pipe cleaner for legs and a long piece for the tail. Curl the tail piece around a pencil.

Caterpillar

You will need four or more pom-poms, all the same size. Tie them together in pairs and glue the pairs together. Glue on a face and use pipe cleaners for the antennae.

Owl

Make one small and one medium-sized pom-pom. Knot them together. Glue on two big yellow felt eyes with black felt centers. Use a tiny piece of black pipe cleaner for the beak. Glue on small feathers for the wings. If the owl doesn't stand up, trim off some of the yarn from the bottom.

Making a corker

Years ago, families made corkers by hammering four small nails around the top of an empty thread spool. Thread no longer comes on wooden spools, but you can still make a terrific corker. Turn the page to find out how to use it.

Things you need

- a bathroom tissue roll tube
- scissors
- masking tape or colorful cloth tape

- 8 smooth, thin finishing nails about 4 cm (1 1/2 in.) long
- felt or fabric scraps (optional)
- white craft glue
- a rubber band

1 Make a lengthwise cut straight along the tube to open it.

2 Cut six pieces of tape, each about 8 cm (3 in.) long.

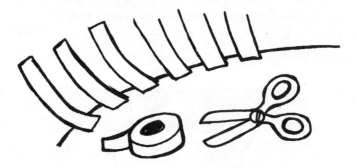

3 Roll the tube until it is doubled around. Attach the strips of tape down the entire length to hold this shape.

4 Cut another strip of tape 10 cm (4 in.) long and place it sticky side out along the top edge of the tube.

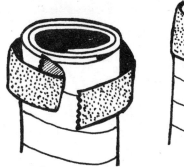

5 Hold two nails side by side and place them on the tape so that 1 cm (½ in.) of the nails is above the top of the tube.

6 Place a second pair of nails across from the first pair. Place two more pairs of nails across from each other so that you have four evenly spaced pairs of nails around the top of your tube.

7 Use more tape to cover the nails and the sticky side of the tape along the top. Cut four narrow pieces of tape and place them in the spaces between the pairs of nails to help hold the nails in place.

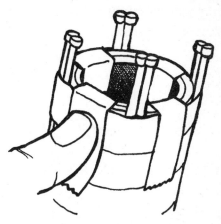

8 You can decorate your corker by wrapping colorful cloth tape around it or by gluing on a piece of felt or fabric.

9 Place the rubber band around the middle of your corker as a handy spot to tuck your corking needle (see the next page) when you are not using it.

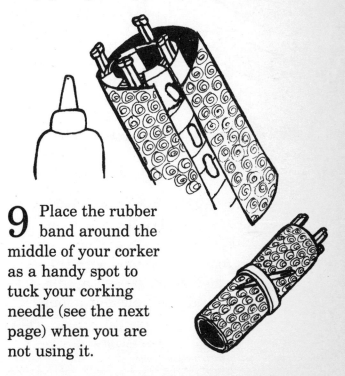

Corking

Whether you call it spool knitting, knitting knobby, knitting Nancy or Bizzy Lizzy, corking is a fun, treasured old-time craft you can do anywhere, anytime.

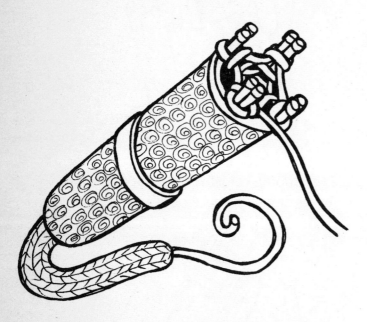

Things you need

- a corker (available at craft and hobby stores, or see page 170 for how to make your own)
- a corking tool (often comes with the corker, or you can use a yarn needle, a plastic cocktail toothpick, or a long, thin nail)
- a ball of yarn • scissors

1 Make a slip knot about 25 cm (10 in.) from the end of the yarn. Place the knot loop over a peg (or set of nails if you are using a homemade corker). Poke the yarn tail down the center of the corker.

2 Bring the yarn from the ball behind the next peg, wind it around this peg and bring it behind the next peg. Repeat on the next two pegs so that all the pegs have yarn looped around them. Hold the corker in either hand and wind the yarn either way, as long as you don't change directions in the middle of a project.

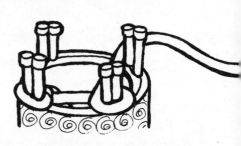

3 You should now have the yarn back to the peg with the slip knot on it. Wind the yarn in front of this peg, above the slip knot loop. Hold the yarn end in place with the fingers holding the corker.

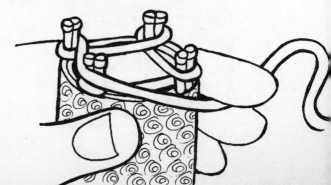

4 Poke the corking tool down into the slip knot loop, being careful not to split the yarn. Pull the yarn loop towards you and lift it up and over the top line of yarn and the peg. Let it off your needle.

5 Turn the corker as you wind the yarn above the loops on the pegs. Continue to lift the bottom yarn over the top, keeping your stitches loose. Every once in a while pull down on the yarn tail hanging out the bottom.

6 To change colors, cut off the yarn you are using, leaving a 5-cm (2-in.) tail. Knot the new color to the old one and keep corking. Tuck the knot into the center of the corking so it doesn't show.

7 To finish off, cut the yarn, leaving a 20-cm (8-inch) tail. Lift the loop off the peg you just corked and put it on the next peg. Do a regular corking stitch. Lift the leftover loop and put it on the next peg, and so on until you are left with one loop on one peg.

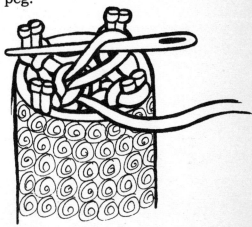

8 Pull on the last loop to make it larger. Thread the yarn tail through it and pull it tight as you lift it off the peg.

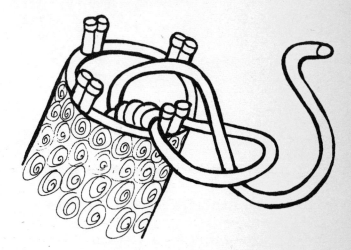

9 Turn the page for what to make with your corking.

A corker of a pot holder

Get busy corking and, before you know it, you'll have enough to make this pot holder or any of the other ideas on these pages.

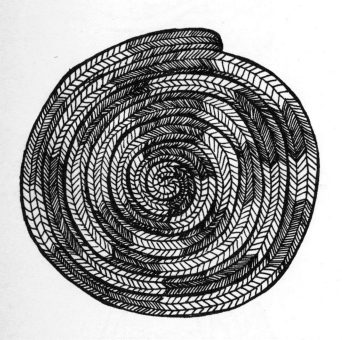

Things you need

- 2 m (6 ½ ft.) of corking (see page 172)
- yarn
- a yarn needle
- scissors

1 Cut an arm length of yarn. Knot the yarn at one end and thread it into the needle.

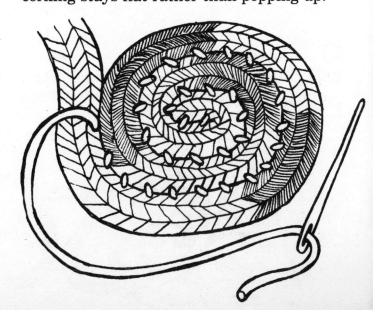

2 Bend the corking into a short, tight J. Pull the needle through a couple of stitches from each part of the J. The stitches should not show on the front of your work. Wind the corking around some more.

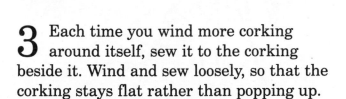

3 Each time you wind more corking around itself, sew it to the corking beside it. Wind and sew loosely, so that the corking stays flat rather than popping up.

4 When you reach the end of the corking (or run out of yarn), make a couple of stitches in the same spot and weave the yarn into the corking so it doesn't show. Trim any yarn ends.

Sew a length of corking about 45 cm (18 in.) long into a circle for an easy hair band. Make many in different colors so you'll have lots ready for gifts.

More ideas

Use your pot holder for a dollhouse mat or set a plant on it.

Make a small pot holder to use as a coaster. You will need about 75 cm (30 in.) of corking.

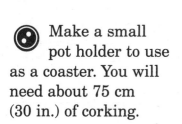

Corking is a great way to use up leftover yarn. See how many different colors of yarn you can get into your length of corking. By the time you run out of yarn, you may have enough corking to make yourself a bedside mat!

For an oval pot holder or placemat, sew the corking together in a long, narrow U shape. Continue to wind and sew the corking in this oval shape.

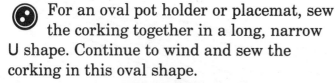

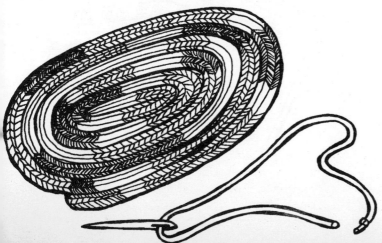

Weaving loom

This loom is large enough for weaving placemats. Use the same method, but a much smaller piece of cardboard and closer-spaced notches, to make a loom suitable for weaving coasters, bookmarks and other small items.

1 Cut a rectangle of cardboard about 55 cm x 40 cm (22 in. x 16 in.). Also cut two strips of cardboard, each about 4 cm x 40 cm (1 1/2 in. x 16 in.). Near the end of one strip, cut a long triangular-shaped indent into each side. This strip will be your bobbin and the other strip your heddle for weaving.

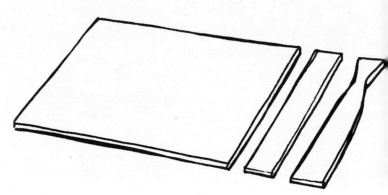

2 Draw a line along each end of the large cardboard, 1.5 cm (5/8 in.) in from the edge. Starting on the left side, make a mark every 1 cm (3/8 in.) along the line.

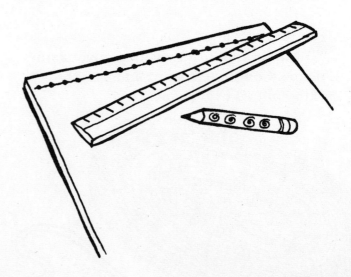

Things you need

- sturdy, corrugated cardboard
- a ruler
- a pencil
- scissors or an X-acto knife

3 Turn the cardboard so the other short end is in front of you. This time start at the right side and make a mark every 1 cm (³/₈ in.) along the line.

5 Now make angled cuts from the edges to the marks so you are cutting out small triangles and making jagged teeth.

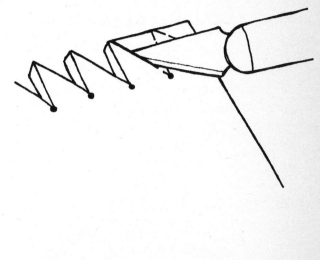

4 At each end make short, straight cuts from the edge of the cardboard to the marks.

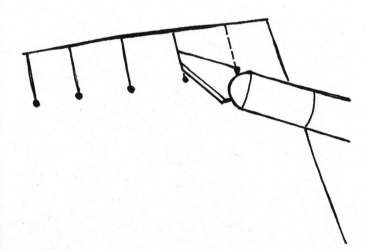

6 If your cardboard has a few bends in it after all the measuring and cutting, glue a slightly smaller rectangle onto the back. (Make sure it does not interfere with the teeth on each end.) Place a few heavy books on it to dry.

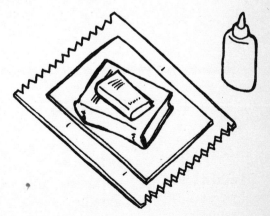

7 Turn the page to find out how to use your loom.

Woven placemats

Weave a pair of placemats for a special pair of people using your homemade loom.

Things you need

- a cardboard loom (see page 176)
- a ball of cotton knitting worsted yarn
- tape
- scissors
- a large, blunt yarn needle

1 Tape the yarn end to the back of your loom. Starting at the second notch, wind the yarn around the loom. The yarn should not be taut or too loose. When you reach the other side, cut the yarn and tape it to the back of the loom. These are your warp threads.

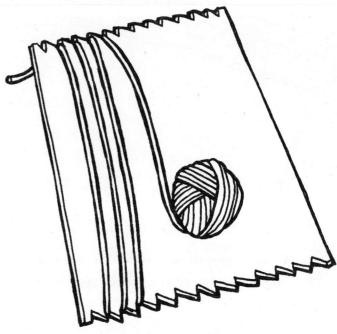

2 Wind lots of yarn around the cutout area of the bobbin.

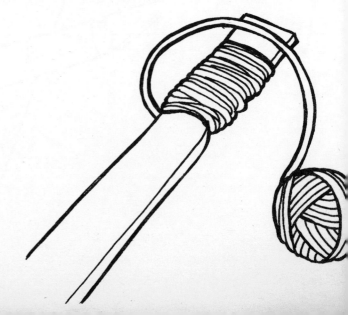

3 Weave the heddle over, then under, the warp threads near the center of the loom. Turn it up so it lifts every second warp thread.

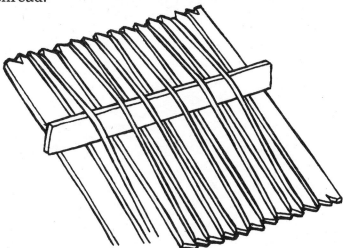

5 Unwind some thread from your bobbin and weave it back to the left side, going over the warp threads you went under before, and under the threads you went over before. Push this weft thread close to the first one with the heddle.

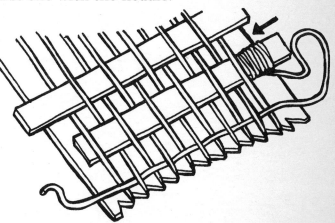

4 Starting at the bottom left corner of the loom, slide the bobbin under the raised warp threads across to the right side. (Leave a thread tail hanging at the left side to be woven in later.) This is the weft thread. Turn the heddle down and use it to push the weft thread to the bottom of the loom.

6 When you are back at the left side, turn the heddle between the warp threads upright again, unwind some thread from the bobbin and pass it between the threads.

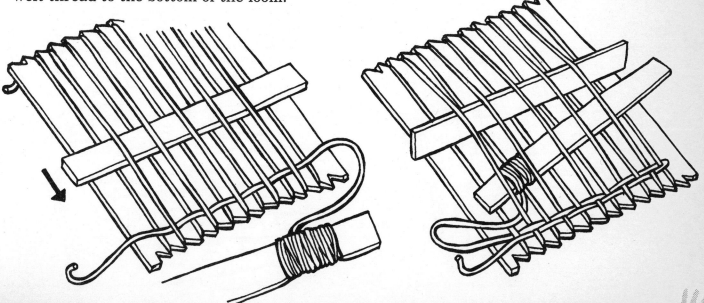

Continued on next page

7 Keep going back and forth, with one quick crossing and the other weaving a little slower. Keep the side loops loose so your placemat does not go in at the sides. Push each new weft thread against the one before.

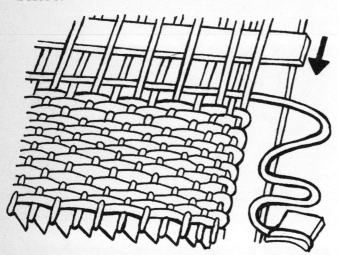

9 To remove the placemat from the loom, cut the warp threads at the back. Tie each warp thread to the one beside it using an overhand knot. This will create a fringe. Trim all the fringe threads evenly.

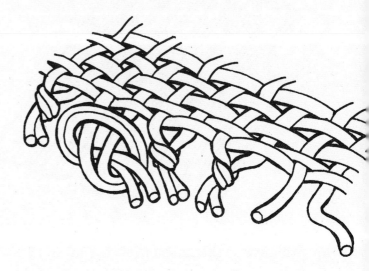

8 If you run out of yarn, leave the tail thread at the side, re-thread your bobbin and continue, again leaving a tail at the side.

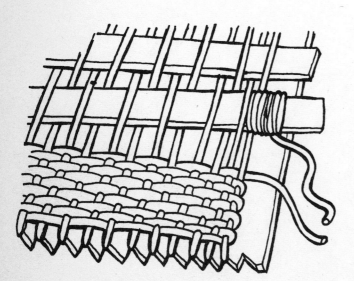

10 Use the yarn needle to weave in all the side tail pieces, going over and under five warp threads.

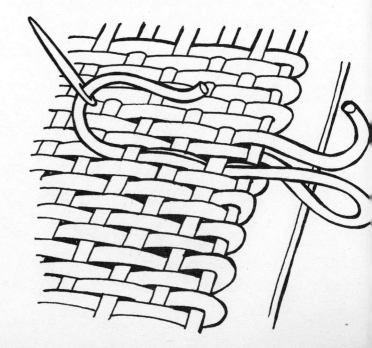

More ideas

Try using different colors for the warp threads and the weft threads.

Weave stripes. Make as many bobbins as you have colors of yarn and keep changing colors. Always leave tails at the beginning and end of each stripe to be woven in later.

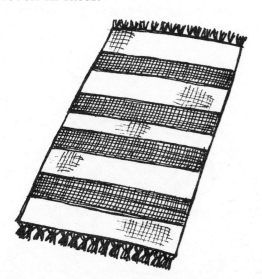

You can use regular yarn on your loom. It is stretchier than cotton yarn, so be careful not to pull it too tight.

For a more tightly woven placemat, make more notches on the ends of your loom. You can also use crochet cotton for a finer weave. A finely woven placemat can be stenciled for a fabulous finishing touch (see page 182). If you make a small loom with many notches, try threading it with crochet cotton to make a bookmark. This bookmark would be perfect for stenciling, too, or make it striped.

For a very different look, weave in narrow strips of fabric. You'll have more tails to weave in, but your placemat will be finished quicker.

Stenciling

Stenciling is an old-time craft that is still used to decorate everything from a pillowcase to a wooden stool or a wall. It allows you to repeat a design without having to draw it over and over again. Check wallpaper and fabric patterns to get ideas for designing your stencil.

Things you need

- a pen
- a plastic lid from a margarine or yogurt tub
- an X-acto knife
- a piece of corrugated cardboard
- a washed plain pillowcase, napkin or other fabric item
- masking tape
- non-toxic paint sticks
- a stenciling brush

1 Draw a design on the shiny side of the plastic lid. You can experiment on paper first, but since ink will rub off the plastic, you can draw directly on it.

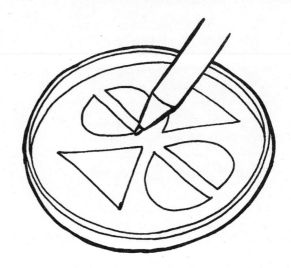

2 Place the lid on the cardboard and ask an adult to help you cut out the design with the X-acto knife. Cut away the outer rim too. This is your stencil.

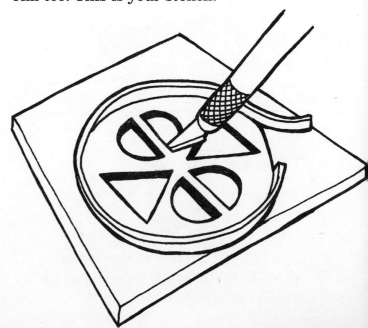

3 Tape the fabric item to your work surface, making sure it is smooth.

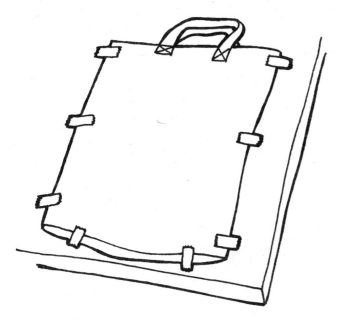

4 Tape the stencil in place on the fabric. Draw a line of paint with a paint stick around every edge of your design. (You may need to remove the dry paint coating that forms on new sticks or on any stick when it hasn't been used for a day or more.)

5 Use a sweeping motion with the brush to move the paint from the stencil to the fabric. Always sweep towards the center of each cutout area. Stenciling looks best when there are light and dark areas of color, so you don't need to fill the shape in evenly.

6 When you are pleased with the amount of paint on the fabric, lift the stencil and tape it down on another area. Be careful not to put tape on the fresh paint.

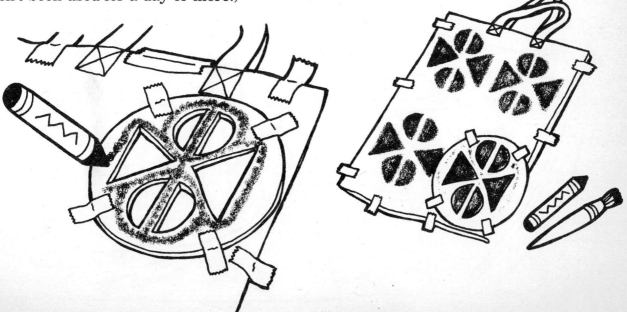

Continued on next page

7 If you want to change the paint color, wipe the stencil clean with a rag. Wash the brush with soap and water and make sure it is dry before you start again. (It's handy to have another stenciling brush so you won't have to keep washing the same brush.)

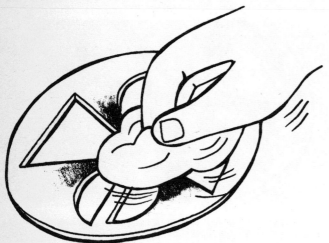

8 Let the paint dry for 24 hours. Then cover the area with a dry cloth and iron it to set the paint. (Or follow the manufacturer's instructions on the paint stick.)

More ideas

⬤ Stencil a card, a gift box, wrapping paper or a wooden item. Don't use tape on paper items — just hold the stencil firmly in place.

⬤ To stencil a clay pot or other curved item, use a lighter material such as a sheet of clear plastic used for overhead projectors. Tape it in place and continue.

🔘 Prepare a T-shirt for stenciling by putting a piece of cardboard inside to keep it smooth.

🔘 Cut two stencils that you can use together, such as a flower and leaves. One stencil would have the petals and the other would have the stem and leaves. Use one and then the other, each with a different-colored paint.

🔘 If you wish to use liquid paint, dip in the brush and dab most of the paint off on a tray or rag. Gently dab the brush over the stencil, being careful not to get any under the edges.

Victorian yarn doll

Years ago, often the only way a child could have a doll was to make one. Since most families had some yarn around, a yarn doll was a good and inexpensive one to make.

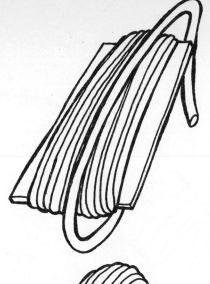

1. Wind yarn around the cardboard about 20 times for thick yarn or 50 times for regular yarn.

2. Gently slide the yarn off the cardboard.

3. To make hair, cut a 50-cm (20-in.) piece of yarn and knot it a little down from the top. Let the ends hang down the back.

4. Knot another 50-cm (20-in.) piece of yarn below the hair to form the head. Again let the ends hang down the back.

5. Cut all the loop ends on the bottom of the doll.

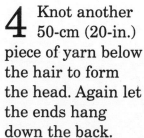

Things you need

- a piece of sturdy cardboard 25 cm x 15 cm (10 in. x 6 in.)
- yarn
- scissors
- a ruler
- decorating supplies such as beads, roly eyes, felt, ribbon and embroidery floss

6 Separate some of the strands of yarn from the sides of the doll to make arms. Tie them in an overhand knot and trim off the extra yarn.

More ideas

◉ Tie the hands together in front and tuck in some dried or silk flowers.

◉ Cut out a large felt heart and glue it to the back to make angel wings. Add a tinsel pipe-cleaner halo.

7 Tie the waist with a piece of yarn and let the ends hang down the back.

◉ After separating the yarn for the arms, braid the body, tie the waist and braid the legs. Braid the arms, too.

◉ Use beads, felt, roly eyes or embroidery floss to make a face.

8 Leave the remaining yarn loose to make a skirt or separate it into two parts to make legs. Tie them at the feet. Trim off any uneven strands of yarn.

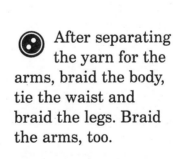

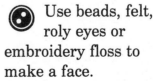

Old-fashioned hanky doll

Before disposable tissues came on the scene, most people carried a handkerchief in their pocket. It came in handy to wipe a nose, dry a tear or make into a lovely doll.

Things you need

- a clean handkerchief or hemmed piece of cotton, about 40 cm (16 in.) square
- polyester fiber stuffing
- a rubber band
- white craft glue
- gathered lace
- ribbon

1 Lay the handkerchief flat on the table, good side down.

2 Put some stuffing about the size of your fist a hand width down from the top.

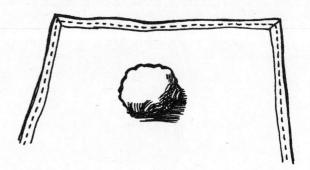

3 Use the rubber band to fasten the stuffing in the handkerchief.

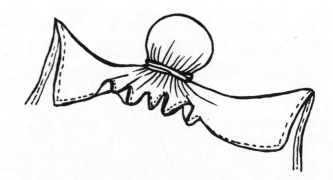

4 Tie knots in the top two corners of the handkerchief to make arms.

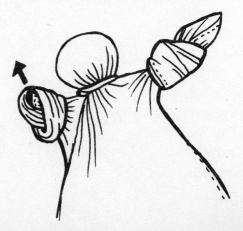

5 Apply glue in a circle around your doll's face.

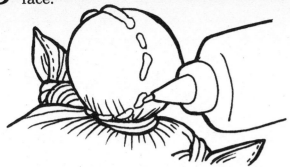

6 Place the lace over the glue to make a bonnet. Hold it until the glue begins to dry.

7 Tie the ribbon around the doll's neck to cover the rubber band.

8 Traditionally, a doll like this does not have a face, but give yours one, if you like.

More ideas

🔘 Make a handkerchief doll out of a colorful bandanna.

🔘 Make legs on your doll by tying knots in the bottom corners, too.

🔘 Sew or glue on gathered lace along the bottom edge.

🔘 Embroider your initials in one of the bottom corners. Also, try a row or two of other embroidery stitches along the bottom (see page 202).

Hand puppet

Once you've made a puppet pattern, you can use it to create many characters. Simply change the color of the felt, the size and shape of the ears, add spots or stripes, clothing or whatever else you can think of.

Things you need

- paper and a pencil
- scissors
- felt
- buttons and other materials for face
- a darning needle
- yarn
- pins
- white craft glue (optional)

1 Put your hand on the paper and draw a wide outline around your hand and wrist as shown. Make sure the bottom is very wide.

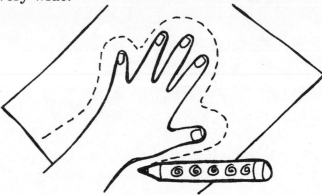

2 Cut this paper pattern out.

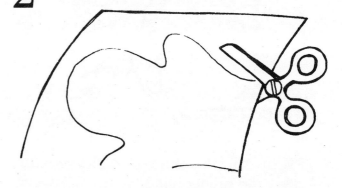

3 Trace your pattern twice onto the felt with a pencil. Use chalk or a dried sliver of soap if your felt is a dark color.

4 Cut out the two felt shapes.

5 Sew on button eyes and stitch the rest of the face. If you decide to glue on the face, you can do it at the end.

6 Pin the two felt shapes together. If your puppet needs ears, cut them out and pin them in between the two layers of felt.

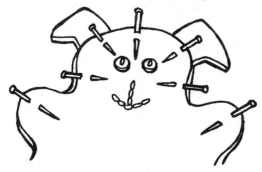

7 Sew the puppet together. Remove the pins as you sew. Leave the bottom open.

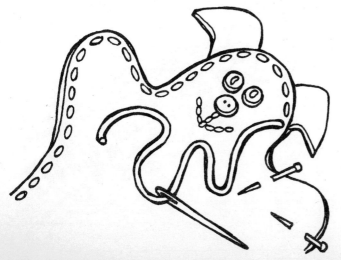

More ideas

● Sew or glue on paws, a bow-tie, hair, clothing, roly eyes, whiskers or a hat to create a whole new character.

● Make your hand puppet out of fabric. Use pinking shears to cut it out.

Button buddy

It used to be that every family had a button box. If you don't have one, buttons are available at fabric and craft supply stores.

Things you need

- 2 pipe cleaners, one 30 cm (12 in.) long, one 15 cm (6 in.) long
- about 10 medium-sized buttons and 1 large one
- a wooden bead
- a permanent marker
- yarn

1 Fold the long pipe cleaner in half and thread the large button onto it. This button is your doll's hat.

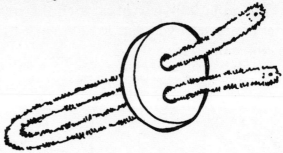

2 Thread the bead head onto both ends of the pipe cleaner.

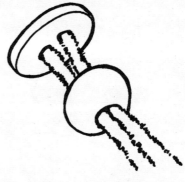

3 Thread the rest of the buttons onto the pipe cleaner to make the body.

4 Twist the legs twice under the last button so the buttons cannot fall off.

5 For the arms, wind the short pipe cleaner between two of the buttons near the top.

6 Fold back the ends of the pipe cleaners to make hands and feet.

7 Draw a face on your button buddy and watch it come to life!

8 For hair, cut two strands of yarn, tuck them under the button hat and tie them tightly at the back. Untwist the strands of yarn for wavy hair.

More ideas

⊙ Run a length of yarn or thin ribbon under the pipe cleaner on top of your doll's button hat to hang it up.

⊙ Make a baby button buddy by using shorter pieces of pipe cleaner and little buttons.

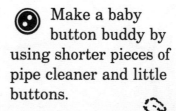

Jointed teddy bear

You can make this teddy out of denim or a fabric that matches your bedroom. This bear is not suitable for very young children because of the button joints.

Things you need

- paper and a pencil
- scissors
- white craft glue
- thin cardboard
- sturdy fabric or fleece
- a fabric marker or chalk pencil
- fabric scissors
- pins
- a needle, thread and thimble

- 4 medium-sized, two-hole buttons
- polyester fiber stuffing
- a dollmaker's needle (long and strong)
- embroidery floss
- satin ribbon
- a sewing machine (optional)

1 Trace the pattern pieces shown on these pages. Cut them out and glue them onto thin cardboard. Cut them out again.

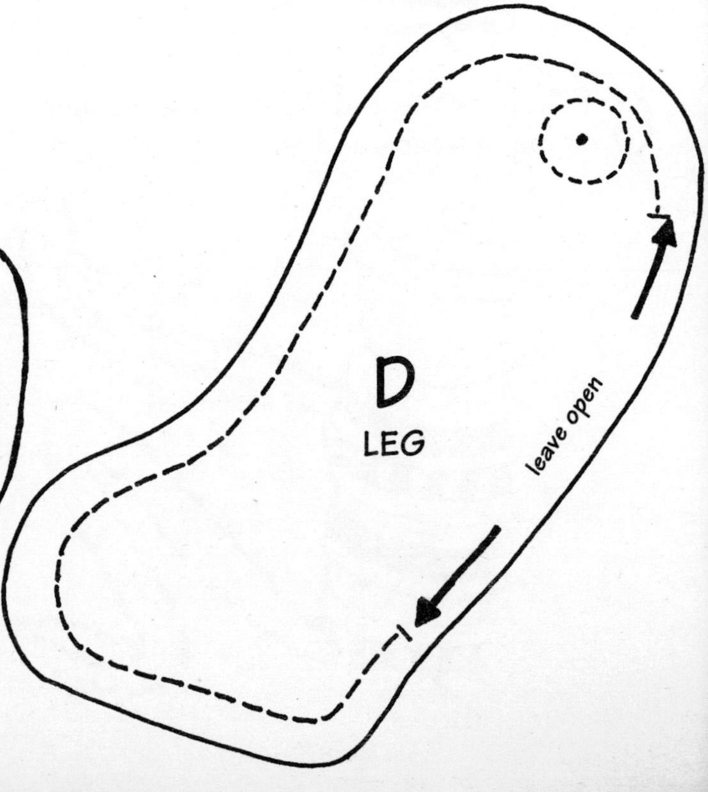

D
LEG

leave open

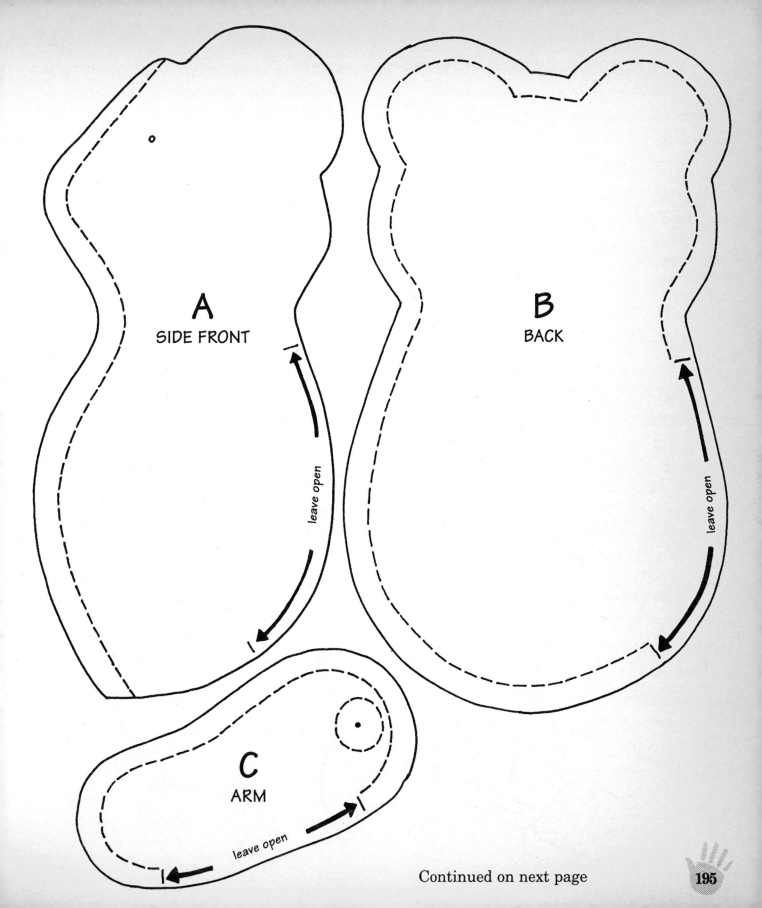

A

SIDE FRONT

leave open

B

BACK

leave open

C

ARM

leave open

Continued on next page

2 Trace your pattern pieces onto the fabric as follows:

A — trace one, flip the pattern over and trace another one

B — trace one

C — trace two, flip the pattern over and trace two more

D — trace two, flip the pattern over and trace two more.

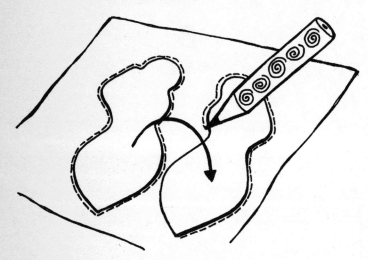

3 Cut out all eleven pieces.

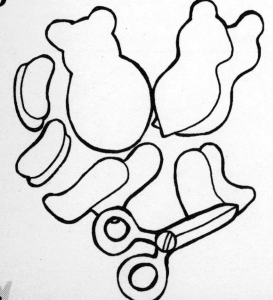

4 All the seams are 0.5 cm (¼ in.) wide. If you like, you can mark the seam allowance on your fabric pieces as well as marking openings and button placements.

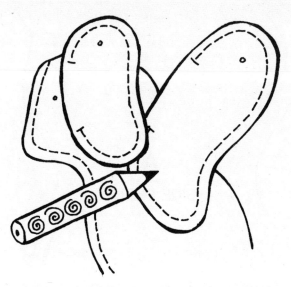

5 Pin the right sides of the side front pieces (A pieces) together, not including the ears. Backstitch (see page 202) the center front seam. Remove the pins as you sew.

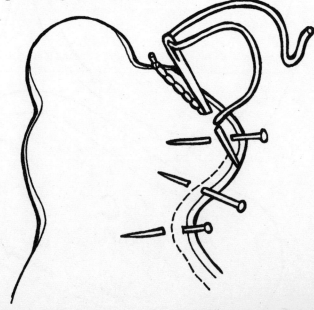

6 Open the front and pin it to the back (B). Stitch all around the outside, except for an opening as marked on the pattern.

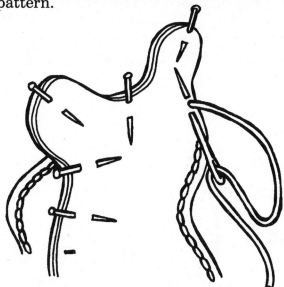

7 Turn the bear body right side out. Poke out the nose and ears with a closed pair of scissors. Set the body aside.

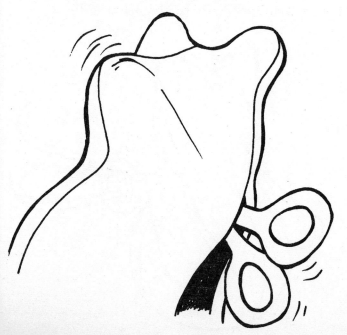

8 With the right sides together, pin the matching arm pieces in pairs. Stitch them, except for the opening as marked on the pattern.

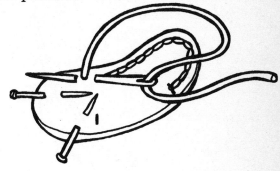

9 Pin and stitch the legs together, too.

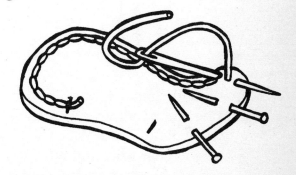

10 Turn the arms and legs right side out. Poke out the corners and stuff them firmly. Tuck in the raw edges and stitch the openings closed.

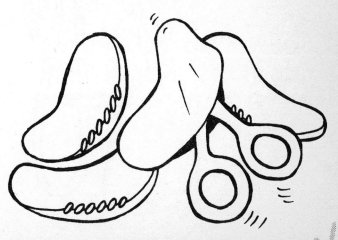

Continued on next page

11 Firmly stuff the head and body, starting with the ears and nose. When your bear looks well rounded, tuck in the raw edges on the side and stitch the opening closed.

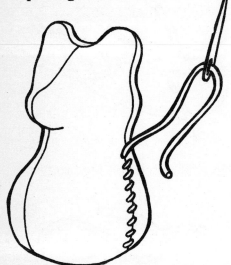

13 Push one arm onto the tip of the needle and draw the needle and floss through the arm. Thread on a button and push the needle back through the button and arm to the other shoulder.

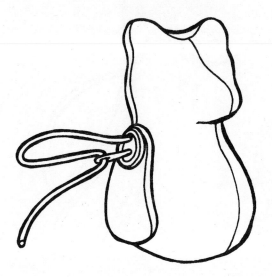

12 Thread the dollmaker's needle with about one and a half arm lengths of embroidery floss. Knot the end. Poke the needle in at one shoulder area and push it through the body so the tip is sticking out at the other shoulder area.

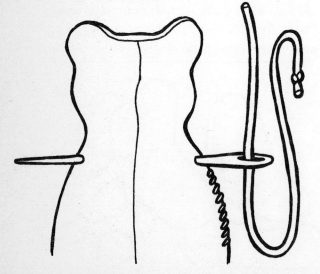

14 Push the other arm onto the tip of the needle and draw the needle and floss through this arm. Thread on another button and push the needle through the button, arm and body to the other side.

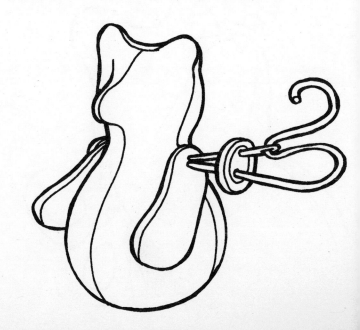

15 Continue back and forth until the buttons are securely fastened on. Make a couple of small stitches under one of the arms, knot the thread and trim it.

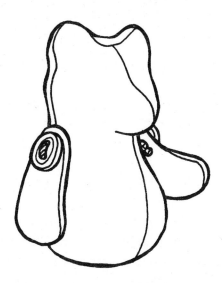

17 Stitch on a face. See page 202 for embroidery ideas. Try cross stitch for the eyes, satin stitch for the nose and backstitch for the mouth and claws. If you'd rather, you can use fabric paint, buttons, beads or felt to make the face.

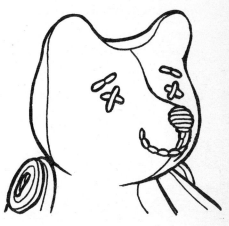

16 Fasten on the legs in the same way. When you have finished, you will be able to move your bear's arms and legs up and down. It is best not to move them around in circles.

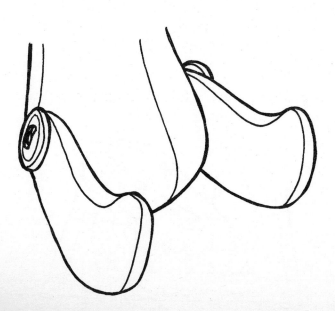

18 For a finishing touch, add a bow tie, paint on a heart, tie on a ribbon, or stitch on buttons. Sit your new bear on your bed or shelf, or wrap it up to give as a gift.

Try using two colors of fabric to create a two-tone teddy!

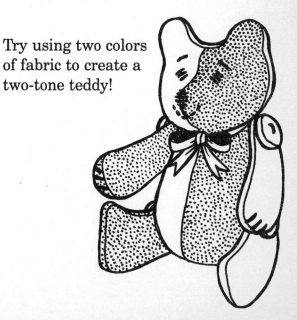

Embroidery

Embroidery is the traditional art of decorating fabric with stitches. It can be done on anything from a pillowcase to jeans, a hat, a vest or a T-shirt. These instructions will give you ideas for embroidering a piece of fabric that can be framed or made into a pillow.

Things you need

- light-colored woven fabric (cotton, linen, broadcloth — ask at a fabric or craft store for suitable fabric if you don't have any)
- masking tape
- paper and a pencil
- a fabric marker or dressmaker's carbon paper and two straight pins
- a few colors of embroidery floss
- a crewel or embroidery needle with an eye large enough for the floss, but small enough to go through the fabric easily
- a 15 to 18 cm (6 to 7 in.) embroidery hoop (optional, but recommended if your fabric is flimsy)

1 Cut a piece of fabric about 25 cm (10 in.) square. Bind the edges with masking tape.

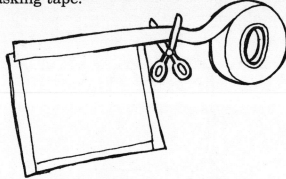

2 On paper, draw or trace a simple picture that will fit on the center area of your fabric. If you're not ready to stitch a picture, use your paper to plan a practice sampler. (A sampler is a piece of fabric that shows many different stitches. It often includes the alphabet, numbers, initials and dates.)

3 If you have a fabric marker, copy your picture onto your fabric.

4 If you are using dressmaker's carbon paper, place it face down on the fabric. Place your picture face up on the carbon paper. Pin the three layers together in the upper two corners. Use a pencil to trace firmly over your picture. Unpin the layers.

5 Cut an arm length of embroidery floss. Thread it into your needle and pull on the floss so the strands are uneven. Knot the long strand.

6 If you are using an embroidery hoop, loosen the tension screw on the outer ring. Place the inner ring on the table and center your fabric square on it. Place the outer ring on top and slide it down. Tighten the screw, but don't pull too much on the fabric or it will stretch out of shape.

7 If you are making a sampler, try each stitch on your fabric (see page 202). Use the threads in the fabric weave as guides to stitch straight rows. If you are embroidering a picture, decide which stitch you will use for each part of your picture.

8 When you are finished, embroider your name and the date on your work. Have it framed or make it into a pillow. To make a pillow, place it good side down on the good side of another piece of fabric the same size. Stitch around the sides except for an opening so it can be turned right side out and stuffed. Stitch the opening closed.

Embroidery stitches

The running stitch and backstitch can be used for regular sewing projects with thread. When stitched with embroidery floss they, as well as the chain stitch, are great for lines and outlines. The cross stitch is good for filling in large areas, while the satin stitch is used for filling in small areas. The lazy-daisy stitch is great for flowers. Knot the thread to begin each stitched area. To finish, bring the thread to the back of the fabric, run it under a few other stitches, knot it and trim it.

Running stitch

Bring the needle up through the fabric and back down beside where your needle came up. Keep pulling the needle up and back down. Make the spaces and stitches even and not too tight.

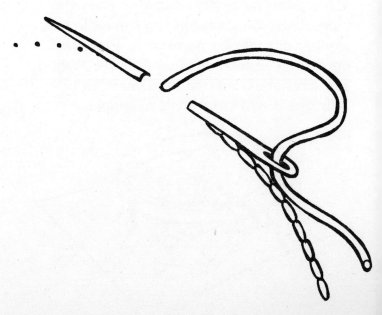

Backstitch

1. Bring the needle up through the fabric and back down near the first stitch. Come up through the fabric again.

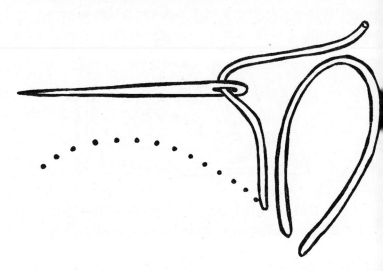

2. Poke the needle into the fabric at the end of the first stitch. Bring the needle out again in front of the thread and pull it through. Keep the stitches even.

Cross stitch

1. Pull the needle through to the good side of the fabric and poke it back down so it makes a diagonal stitch.

2. Bring the needle back up directly below the place where you just poked in the needle. Make another diagonal stitch. Continue until you reach the end of the row.

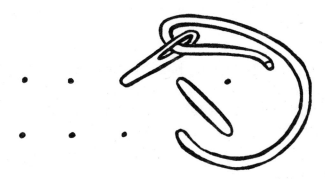

3. To cross these stitches, make diagonal stitches in the opposite direction until you are back where you started.

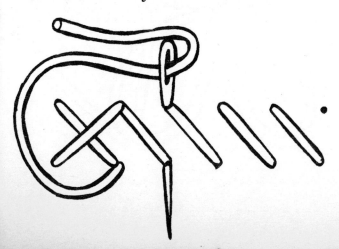

Satin stitch

1. Pull the needle through to the good side of the fabric and poke it back down straight across from where you just came out.

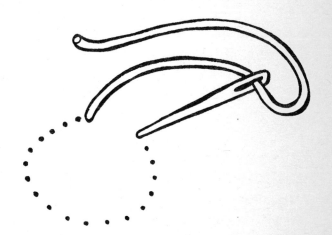

2. Bring the needle back up as close as possible to the first stitch. Again, bring it back down straight across. Keep going until the area is filled in. There should not be any fabric showing between the stitches.

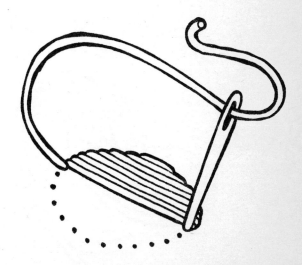

Continued on next page

Chain stitch

1. Pull the needle through to the good side of the fabric. Hold the embroidery floss with your thumb to form a loop. Position the needle so it enters the fabric in the same spot where it just came out. Then poke it through the fabric a small distance across from this point, still inside the loop.

2. Hold the floss under the tip of the needle and pull the needle through the fabric. This will make your first chain stitch. To make more, poke the needle into this same hole and continue as in step 1.

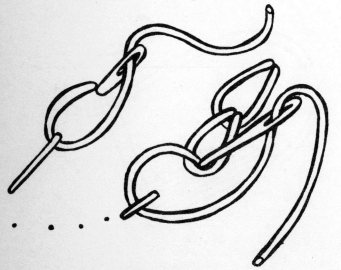

Lazy-daisy stitch

1. Make a chain stitch, but instead of going on to make another one, fasten this one by poking the needle down into the fabric on the other side of the loop.

2. Bring the needle back to the good side of the fabric in the right position to make another chain stitch. Make many in a circular pattern to create a flower.

Index